Developmental Profiles

Pre-birth Through Twelve

4th Edition

Join us on the web at

EarlyChildEd.delmar.com

Developmental Profiles

Pre-birth Through Twelve

4th Edition

K. Eileen Allen
Professor Emerita,
University of Kansas

Lynn R. Marotz, Ph.D., R.N.
University of Kansas

THOMSON

DELMAR LEARNING

Australia   Canada   Mexico   Singapore   Spain   United   Kingdom   United States

155.4
Alle

Developmental Profiles: Pre-birth Through Twelve, 4e
K. Eileen Allen and Lynn R. Marotz

Business Unit Executive Director:
Susan L. Simpfenderfer

Acquisitions Editor:
Erin O'Connor

Developmental Editor
Melissa Riveglia

Executive Production Manager:
Wendy A. Troeger

Production Editor:
Joy Kocsis

Technology Project Manager:
Joseph Saba

Executive Marketing Manager:
Donna J. Lewis

Channel Manager:
Nigar Hale

Cover Design:
Judi Orozco

Composition:
Bookcomp/Nighthawk Design

For permission to use material from this text or product, contact us by
Tel (800) 730-2214
Fax (800) 730-2215
www.thomsonrights.com

Library of Congress Cataloging-in-Publication Data

Allen, K. Eileen, 1918-
  Developmental profiles : pre-birth through twelve / K. Eileen Allen, Lynn R. Marotz.-- 4th ed.
    p. cm.
Includes bibliographical references (p.) and index.
  ISBN 0-7668-3765-3
1. Child development. I. Marotz, Lynn R. II. Title.

RJ131 .A496 2002
155.4--dc21   2002020608

NOTICE TO THE READER

Publisher does not warrant or guarantee any of the products described herein or perform any independent analysis in connection with any of the product information contained herein. Publisher does not assume, and expressly disclaims, any obligation to obtain and include information other than that provided to it by the manufacturer.

The reader is expressly warned to consider and adopt all safety precautions that might be indicated by the activities herein and to avoid all potential hazards. By following the instructions contained herein, the reader willingly assumes all risks in connection with such instructions.

The Publisher makes no representation or warranties of any kind, including but not limited to, the warranties of fitness for particular purpose or merchantability, nor are any such representations implied with respect to the material set forth herein, and the publisher takes no responsibility with respect to such material. The publisher shall not be liable for any special, consequential, or exemplary damages resulting, in whole or part, from the readers' use of, or reliance upon, this material.

Contents

Preface

Developmental Profiles opens with a brief overview of major issues in child development. This serves as a refresher of basic principles and background material for the several chapters on age-level expectancies that follow. The concluding chapters focus on when and where to seek help if there are concerns about a child.

Developmental Profiles is designed for:

■ child development and early childhood students and teachers-in-training
■ teachers in home-based care settings, child care centers, preschools, and Head Start programs, and nannies in the child's own home
■ allied health professionals from fields such as nursing, nutrition, audiology, social work, physical and occupational therapy, psychology, medicine, and language and speech therapy, as well as other disciplines providing services for children and their families
■ parents, the most important contributors to a child's optimum development

Developmental Profiles provides nontechnical information about:

■ what to expect of young children at each succeeding stage of development
■ the ways in which all areas of development are intertwined and mutually supportive
■ the unique pathway that each child follows in a developmental process that is alike, yet different, among children of similar age
■ sequences, not age, being the critical concept in evaluating developmental progress
■ the use of developmental norms in teaching, observing, and assessing children and in designing individualized as well as group learning experiences

Developmental Profiles includes a number of special features:

■ a section that briefly defines and describes the most commonly encountered terms and concepts in the child development literature
■ concise profiles of developmental domains at various age levels from pre-birth through age twelve

■ developmental alerts for each level; that is, signals that may indicate a possible delay or problem

■ descriptions of daily activities and routines typical of children at each level

■ where and how to get help if there is concern about a child's development

■ Web addresses at the end of each chapter for ease in locating professional organizations and additional information resources

■ objectives and key terms to draw the reader's attention to important points in each chapter

■ suggested activities for promoting children's curiosity and learning

■ developmental checklists for use in observing and screening children's developmental progress

■ safety alerts for each developmental stage to help parents and teachers provide safer environments and improved supervision

■ developmental sketches and related questions to help readers link chapter content to real-life situations

■ new photographs to illustrate key concepts described throughout the book

■ an annotated bibliography for backup and additional readings on child development, screening and assessment, diversity, parenting, and referral and information resources

■ color inserts highlighting child and family diversity and observing children in natural environments

■ a sample health history form, examples of frequently used screening and assessment instruments designed for evaluating children from six months through twelve years, and additional resources for families and professionals

ANCILLARIES

Instructor's Manual

The instructor's manual includes answers to the developmental sketch application and review questions located at the end of each chapter. Additional short answer, true/false, and matching test questions are provided, along with a complete answer key.

Computerized Test Bank

The computerized test bank is comprised of true/false, multiple-choice, short answer, and completion questions for each chapter. Instructors can use the computerized test bank software to create sample quizzes for students. Refer to the CTB User's Guide for more information on how to create and post quizzes to your school's Internet or Intranet server. Students may also access sample quizzes from the

Online Resources™ to accompany this fourth edition of *Developmental Profiles: Pre-birth Through Twelve.*

Online Resources™

The Online Resources™ to accompany the 4th edition of *Developmental Profiles: Pre-birth Through Twelve* is your link to early childhood education on the Internet. The Online Resources™ includes many features and resources to help focus and enhance an understanding of child development.

 The Online Resources™ icon appears at the end of each chapter to prompt you to go online and take advantage of the many features provided.

You can find the Online Resources™ at www.earlychilded.delmar.com.

The authors and Delmar Learning make every effort to ensure that all Internet resources are accurate at the time of printing. However, due to the fluid, time-sensitive nature of the Internet, we cannot guarantee that all URLs and Web site addresses will remain current for the duration of this edition.

Introduction

This fourth edition of *Developmental Profiles: Pre-birth through Twelve* has been expanded and updated. At the same time, it maintains the authors' original intent: to provide a comprehensive yet nontechnical, easy-to-follow guide to development. Major characteristics of each developmental domain for each age level continue to be in the original point-by-point format (Chapters 4 through 8). This arrangement has proven invaluable for teachers, students, parents, and practitioners in readily accessing needed information. The Daily Routines for each age are easily located in the shaded boxes. The shading allows Routines to be quickly distinguished from Learning Activities, Developmental Alerts, and new Safety Alerts, which are also noted. Glossary words, as in early editions, are in bold type throughout the text with each term defined at the bottom of the page on which it is used, as well as in a comprehensive glossary at the end of the book.

FEATURES OF THE FOURTH EDITION

Several new features have been added to this fourth edition in an effort to clarify, update, and expand the information presented. For it is teachers—parents, families, and professional teachers—who, through their understanding of the critical importance of the early years, creation of enriched learning opportunities, and modeling of desirable behaviors, ultimately make a difference in children's lives.

Objectives and Key Terms

These pedagogical features draw the reader's attention to important concepts the authors have addressed in each chapter. Objectives are designed to provoke critical thinking. Key terms are highlighted in bold in the text, defined on the page where they first appear, listed at the end of the chapters, and included in a comprehensive glossary at the end of the book.

Developmental Sketches

Developmental Sketches, a new feature in this fourth edition, have been added in shaded boxes to each chapter to promote improved understanding of sometimes complex information. Their placement at the beginning of the chapters is intended to set the stage and encourage readers to analyze and synthesize content as it is presented. Questions, at the end of the chapter, provide readers with an opportunity to apply what they have learned to real-life situations.

Safety Alerts

Because children are always at greater risk of injury, the authors felt strongly that more information on safety promotion should be included in this latest edition. Safety Concerns highlight some of the most important safety considerations at each age-developmental stage. Suggestions are based on the rapidly occurring changes in children's growth and development which, in turn, have a direct effect on the nature of adult awareness and supervision necessary.

Prenatal Development (Chapter 3)

New material has been included in the revision of this chapter to reflect current research and to help students, teachers, parents, and practitioners better understand the process of fetal development. Month-by-month developments in fetal growth are described in a concise, visual format. Additional information on nutrition, maternal infections, and drugs that may potentially interfere with healthy fetal development has also been provided, along with several new tables for easy reference.

Developmental Profiles for Nine-, Ten-, Eleven-, and Twelve-Year-Olds

The age span covered in the previous edition has now been expanded to include middle childhood. This decision is an effort to respond to the expressed needs of the many early childhood professionals who work with before- and after-school programs, as well as parents who are always interested in their children's developmental progress. Because there is considerable overlap in development during this period, profiles have been grouped and presented in two separate categories: nine- and ten-year-olds; and eleven- and twelve-year-olds.

As always, the authors sound the warning that age-level expectancies are based on averaging the behaviors and achievements of large numbers of children of similar age and background in each area of development. Thus, even typically developing children, in real life, may vary greatly from the norms due to individual differences in genetic makeup, environments, and personal experiences.

Full-Color Inserts on Diversity and Observation of Children

These color inserts have been included to draw the reader's attention to important contemporary issues. One insert focuses on diversity and the implications for teachers, caregivers, and allied practitioners. It showcases the range of cultural, economic, and developmental differences that characterize children and families in schools and child care settings. Another insert addresses the all-important topic of observing children. Emphasis is placed on the value of systematic observation to ensure quality and individualized guidance in early education programs. Several strategies are described that teachers, parents, and students can use when observing children in naturalistic environments, such as home and school.

Chapter 9

Information on when and how to seek help for children who may have, or who are suspected of having, developmental disabilities has been completely revised, expanded, and updated. An annotated sampling of screening and assessment instruments has also been updated and included in Appendix 5. Additional resources for families and professionals, including an expanded list of organizations and special-interest Web sites, is now available in a new appendix (Appendix 6) for easier location and use.

Annotated Bibliography and References

The annotated bibliography (Appendix 8) has been thoroughly updated while retaining titles that have classic status. The authors acknowledge that there are many excellent books available on these topics, but have included only a limited selection due to space considerations.

Helpful Web Sites

Web site addresses for many professional organizations and resources are provided for readers who are interested in accessing additional information relevant to the topics discussed in each chapter. Links to other valuable resources can often be found on these sites.

New Photographs

Throughout the book, many of the line sketches used in previous editions have been replaced by photographs in an effort to update the illustration of fundamental concepts and improve the reader's ability to relate material to contemporary settings and experiences.

PHILOSOPHICAL NOTES

The common practice of dividing infancy and childhood into age-related units of months and years can distort the realities of human development. On the other hand, when describing developmental expectations, developmental progress, and delays, other systems seem to work even less well. Let it be stressed here, as it is again and again throughout the text, that the age specifications are only approximate markers derived from *averages* or *norms*. In a way, they can be thought of as midpoints not intended to represent any one child. Age expectations also can be thought of as summary terms for skills that vary from child to child in form and time of acquisition. The truly important consideration in assessing a child's development is *sequence*. The essential question is not chronological age, but whether the child is moving forward step-by-step in each area of development. *Developmental Profiles* proves itself an invaluable resource in addressing this issue.

As in the three previous editions of *Developmental Profiles*, the early days, weeks, and months of infancy are looked at in great detail. New research findings on brain and early development clearly support the critical importance of this relatively short time span. What is now known about the infant's capacity for learning is indeed amazing given conventional wisdom, which suggests that young babies simply flounder around in a "booming, buzzing" confusion. Far from it! With more and more infants entering infant programs at ever earlier ages, it is most important that teachers are knowledgeable about infant development and learning, and that parents hold appropriate expectations and can describe to teachers what they want and believe is best for their infants.

The first year of life is critical in terms of building a foundation of learning in every area of development. The vast array of new and complex behaviors that toddlers and preschoolers must learn in three or four short years is also monumental. At no other period in a lifetime will so much be expected of an individual in so short a time. With other-than-parent child care being the norm rather than the exception, it is essential that teachers and parents have a thorough knowledge of how young children grow, develop, and learn. Thus, an underlying theme of *Developmental Profiles* continues to be partnership with parents. No matter how many hours a day the child is with caregivers, parents still play the most significant role. They need to be encouraged to talk about their child, and to share their observations and concerns. Such information is integral to the well-being of each child. And always, when parents talk, professionals need to listen with focused attention and respond with genuine respect.

Partnership with parents becomes even more critical when an infant or older child is suspected of having a developmental problem or irregularity. The Developmental Alerts following each age section can be especially useful to either a parent or a teacher in initiating a discussion about their concerns. Let it be emphasized, however, that under no circumstances should this book or any other book be seen as an instrument for diagnosing a developmental problem. That is the job of professional clinicians.

The purposes of this text can be summed up as follows:

- to provide a concise review of developmental principles
- to provide easily accessible information about what to expect at each developmental level
- to suggest appropriate ways for adults to facilitate learning and development during the early years
- to pinpoint warning signs of a possible developmental problem
- to suggest how and where to get help
- to describe cultural and ethnic diversity in terms of its impact on the developmental process
- to emphasize the value of direct observation of children in their natural settings, be it a classroom, a family day care program, or the child's own home
- to help adults encourage every child to achieve his or her potential, develop a positive sense of self-esteem, and to feel loved and respected

Acknowledgments

First and foremost, the authors would like to recognize Delmar Learning's continued commitment to the field of early education. Their foresight and dedicated efforts have contributed to improved parent and teacher understanding of children as unique individuals and opportunities for supporting and enhancing learning. We are especially grateful to Erin O'Connor, Melissa Riveglia, and other Delmar Learning editorial staff members for their hard work and invaluable assistance in the preparation of this fourth edition.

The authors also wish to extend a special thank-you to Michelle Scott, a former student, mother, and early education teacher, for her insightful research and contributions to the Safety Alerts and content on middle childhood. Her perceptiveness and dedication to young children are keenly apparent and an asset to the field of early education.

We also wish to thank Vanja A. Holm, MD, friend and colleague, for sharing her specialized expertise and time to update the information on medical and genetic aspects of early development. Her generosity and enduring commitment to children are admirable.

We also want to express appreciation to our reviewers for their valuable comments and suggestions and always helping us to see issues from multiple perspectives:

Linda Aiken, MA
Southwestern Community College
Sylva, North Carolina

Wendy Sue Bertoli, MEd
Lancaster County Career and Technical Center
Mount Joy, Pennsylvania

Sylvia Brooks
University of Delaware
Newark, Delaware

Claude Endfield
Northland Pioneer College
Holbrook, Arizona

Kathleen Fite, PhD
Southwest Texas State University
San Marcos, Texas

Robin Hasslen, PhD
St. Cloud State University
St. Cloud, Minnesota

Ruth Robinson Saxton, PhD
Georgia State Univerity
Dacula, Georgia

Finally, we would like to thank our readers for their dedication and commitment to improving the quality of life for children and families everywhere.

About the Authors

K. Eileen Allen, professor emerita, was a member of the Early Childhood faculty at the University of Washington in Seattle and at the University of Kansas in Lawrence. For a total of thirty-one years she taught a variety of courses: child development, developmental disabilities in young children, parenting, early education, and an interdisciplinary approach to early intervention and inclusion. She also trained teachers and supervised research-focused classrooms at both schools, and has published seven college textbooks as well as numerous research articles and position papers in major professional journals. During her retirement she continues to write, jury research articles, consult in both the private and public sector, and actively advocate on behalf of children and families.

Lynn R. Marotz is a member of the Department of Human Development and Family Life faculty, and also serves as the Associate Director of the Edna A. Hill Child Development Center at the University of Kansas. She has also been a visiting scholar at Arizona State University. She brings her nursing background, training in education, and years of experience with children to the field of early education. Her primary interests include teacher training and administration, policy development, early identification of health impairments, and the promotion of wellness among young children. She teaches undergraduate and graduate courses in child development, parenting, administration, health, and nutrition. Her experience also includes extensive involvement with state policy development, health screenings, working with parents and allied health professionals, and the referral process. She has made numerous professional presentations at state and national conferences, and has authored a variety of publications on children's health, identification of illness and developmental problems, environmental safety, and nutrition. In addition, she also serves on a number of state and local advisory boards.

Principal Concepts in Child Development

 OBJECTIVES

After reading this chapter, you should be able to:

- List at least five essential needs in children's physical development and in their psychological development.
- Provide a brief sketch of the four major approaches to understanding the developing child, and name the principal proponents of each theory.
- Explain why it is essential to help children build self-respect and self-esteem. Suggest at least five ways to promote these strengths in children.
- Define developmental milestones and give examples of such milestones during infancy.
- Defend this statement: "It is *sequence, not age,* that is the important factor in evaluating a child's progress."

 MEET FOUR-YEAR-OLD JOEL

Joel was an undernourished and severely neglected nine-month-old when first placed in foster care. As a four-year-old, he is now in his fifth foster home, where he has been for almost a year. The foster parents, Berta and Doug Clay, have two little girls of their own, ages four and six, and three other foster children ranging in age from four to nine. The children are vigorous and outgoing. Joel, on the other hand, is an overly thin child who seems to have little energy even though he eats far more than any of the other children. Rarely does Joel join in the children's indoor or outdoor play, and he seldom talks with them or the parents. Yet, when he thinks he is alone, both Berta and Doug have overheard him holding lengthy and comprehensible conversations with himself and with an imaginary *Honey*. The talk is usually about things he fears, possibly the root of the recurring bad dreams from which he often wakes up screaming. Yet, Joel is a lovable child. He now seizes any opportunity to curl up in Berta's or Doug's lap, suck his thumb, and snuggle his free hand into one of theirs. The Clays have come to love Joel as one of their own. Fully aware of the challenges that his current development status presents, they are in the process of formally adopting him.

Child development has been a major research focus of psychology for decades. Throughout the years, there has been ongoing disagreement known as the heredity versus environment (**nature/nurture**) controversy. Coming from both sides of the issue, a long line of researchers provides us with the principal concepts related to how children learn, how they grow, how they mature. Most of our current knowledge stems from research related to four theories: maturational, psychoanalytic, cognitive-developmental, and learning. Following are brief descriptions of each theory and mention of an early dominant figure in each field.

Maturational theory focuses on a biological or *nature* approach to human development. Historically, Arnold Gesell is the significant figure in this area of developmental research. He argued that development is governed primarily by internal forces of biologic and genetic origin.

Psychoanalytic theory implies that much of human behavior is governed by unconscious processes, some present at birth, others that develop over time. Sigmund Freud is the acknowledged originator of psychoanalytic theory.

Cognitive-developmental theory is attributed to Jean Piaget, who theorized that children construct their own knowledge through active exploration of their environment. Four major stages of development occur, according to Piaget, starting in infancy and continuing into the late teens. These stages are referred to as sensorimotor, preoperational concrete operations, and formal operations.

Learning theory, in its modern form, stems from the work of B. F. Skinner, who formulated a *nurture,* or environmental approach. He argued that development, for the most part, is a series of learned behaviors based on an individual's positive and negative interactions with the environment.

Current approaches to explanations of how children grow and develop rarely rest on any one theory exclusively. Each theory has made important contributions to

---

nature/nurture—refers to whether development is primarily due to biological/genetic forces (heredity/nature) or to external forces (environment/nurture).

our understanding of children. The majority of today's researchers dismiss the nature/ nurture question as an improbable "either/or" proposition; human development is not that simplistic. Instead, it is viewed as an interaction of environmental influences and inborn characteristics.

It is essential that parents, caregivers, and teachers understand the principal concepts of child development. Each child's overall developmental and behavioral progress can then be put into both day-by-day and long-term perspective. This two-track focus helps children grow and develop in ways best suited to each as a unique individual.

To assist parents and teachers in understanding the developmental process, we have selected the following key concepts because of their importance and widespread use in the field of child development. As varied as these concepts are, it is necessary to understand and apply all of them in working effectively with infants and children. (This text is not intended as a comprehensive child development text. Instead it is designed to:

- serve as an easily understood review of basic principles in early learning and development
- provide detailed and concise guidelines of growth and development from conception through childhood in each domain
- detail specific ways to promote and support optimal development from infancy to the onset of puberty

Appendix 8 provides a selected bibliography of comprehensive child development texts.)

ESSENTIAL NEEDS

All children, those who are developing normally or typically, those who have developmental disabilities, and those who are at-risk for developing problems, have essential physical and psychological needs in common. These needs must be met if infants and children are to survive, thrive, and develop to their best potential. Many developmental psychologists view the early years as the most critical in the entire life span. Never again will the child grow so rapidly or change so dramatically. During these very early years, children learn all of the many behaviors that characterize the human species—walking, talking, thinking, and socializing. Truly

---

at-risk—term describing children who may be more likely to have developmental problems due to certain predisposing factors, such as low birth weight (LBW), neglect, or maternal drug addiction.

amazing, all of that within the first two or three years! And, never again will the child be so totally dependent on parents, caregivers, and teachers to satisfy the basic needs of life and to provide opportunities for learning.

To discuss **essential needs** in an orderly and logical fashion, they can be separated into physical and psychological needs. However, it must be understood that they are interrelated and interdependent. Meeting a child's physical needs while neglecting psychological needs may lead to developmental problems. The opposite also is true: a child who is physically neglected frequently experiences trouble in learning and getting along with others.

Physical Needs

■ Adequate shelter and protection from harm: violence, neglect, and preventable accidents.

■ Sufficient food that is nutritious and appropriate to the child's age.

■ Adequate clothing and shoes suitable to the climate and season.

■ Preventive health and dental care; treatment of physical and mental conditions as needed; immunizations as prescribed for childhood illnesses.

■ Cleanliness: handwashing, brushing teeth, bathing.

■ Rest and activity, in balance; space for indoor and outdoor play.

Psychological Needs

■ Affection and consistency—**nurturing** parents and teachers who can be depended on to "be there" for the child; Figure 1-1.

■ Security and trust—familiar surroundings with parents and teachers who respond reliably to the needs of the infant and child.

■ **Reciprocal** exchanges—beginning in earliest infancy give-and-take interactions that promote responsiveness in the child.

■ Appropriate adult expectations as to what the child can and cannot do at each level of development.

■ Acceptance and positive attitudes toward whatever cultural, ethnic, language, or developmental differences characterize the child and family.

---

essential needs—refers to basic physical needs such as food, shelter, and safety as well as psychological needs, including love, security, and trust, which are required for survival and healthy development.

nurturing—nurturing includes qualities of warmth, loving, caring, and attention to physical needs.

reciprocal—exchanges between individuals or groups that are mutually beneficial (or hindering).

Figure 1-1 Children need affection and positive attention from adults.

The Need for Opportunities to Learn

■ Play as an essential component of early learning: infants and children need unlimited opportunities to engage in play in all of its many forms with freedom to explore and experiment, with necessary limits clearly stated and consistently maintained; Figure 1-2.

■ Access to **developmentally appropriate** experiences and play materials; Figure 1-3.

■ An appropriate "match" between a child's skill levels and the materials and experiences available so the child is challenged but not excessively frustrated.

■ Errors and failures treated as important steps in the learning process, never as reasons for criticizing or ridiculing a child.

■ Adults who demonstrate in their everyday lives the appropriate behaviors expected of the child, especially in language, social interactions, or ways of handling stress. Remember: parents and teachers are major models of behavior

---

developmentally appropriate—a term used to describe learning experiences that are individualized based on a child's level of skills, abilities, and interests.

Figure 1-2 Children need freedom to explore.

for children. They also are a child's first teachers; children learn more from what adults do than from what they say.

■ Inclusion in an active language "community," especially family and child care, in which the child can learn to communicate through sounds, gestures, signs, and eventually words and sentences (either spoken, signed, or written).

The Need for Respect and Self-Esteem

■ A supportive environment in which the child's efforts are encouraged and approved: "You picked up all your crayons. Good job!"

■ Respect for accomplishments whether small or large, for errors as well as successes: "Look at that! You laced your shoes all by yourself." (No mention of the eyelet that was missed.)

■ Recognition that accomplishment, the "I can do it" attitude, is the major and most essential component of a child's **self-esteem**: "You're really getting good at pouring the juice!"

self-esteem—feelings about one's self-worth.

Figure 1-3 Play is an important avenue for learning.

■ Sincere attention to what the child is doing well; using **descriptive praise** to help the child learn to recognize and respect his or her own accomplishments: "You got your shoes on the right feet all by yourself!"

■ Awareness of the effort and concentration that go into acquiring basic developmental skills; providing positive responses to each small step as a child works toward mastery of a complex skill, such as self-feeding with a spoon: "Right! Just a little applesauce on the spoon so it stays on."

NORMAL OR TYPICAL DEVELOPMENT

The terms *typical* and *normal*, when referring to the developing child, tend to be used interchangeably. They imply that a child is growing, changing, and acquiring the broad range of skills characteristic of the majority of children of similar age

---

descriptive praise—words or actions that describe to a child specifically what she or he is doing correctly or well (as in the above example about shoes).

Figure 1-4 New skills are built on previously learned skills.

within the same culture. However, such a statement oversimplifies the concept. **Normal** or **typical development** also implies:

■ An integrated process governing change in size, **neurological** structure, and behavioral complexity;

■ A **cumulative** or "building block" process in which each new aspect of growth or development includes and builds on earlier changes; each accomplishment is necessary to acquisition of the next set of skills; Figure 1-4;

■ A continuous process of give and take (reciprocity) between the child and the environment, each changing the other in a variety of ways. Example: the three-year-old drops a cup, breaks it, and the parent scolds the child. Both events, the broken cup and parent's displeasure, are environmental changes

---

normal (typical) development—achievement of certain skills according to a fairly predictable sequence, although with many individual variations.
neurological—refers to the brain and nervous system.
cumulative—an add-on process, bit by bit or step by step.

that the child triggered. From this experience the child may learn to hold on more firmly next time, and this constitutes a change in both the child's and the adult's behavior—fewer broken cups, thus less adult displeasure.

A number of other key concepts are closely related to the basic concept of normal development. These include:

Developmental Milestones

Major markers or points of accomplishment are referred to as developmental milestones in tracking the emergence of motor, social, cognitive, and language skills. They show up in somewhat orderly steps and within fairly predictable age ranges. Milestone behaviors are those that typically developing children are likely to display at approximately the same age. For example, almost every child begins to smile socially by ten to twelve weeks, and to speak a first word or two around twelve months. These achievements (social smile, first words) are but two of the many significant behavioral indications that a child's developmental progress is on track. The failure of one or more developmental milestones to appear within a reasonable time frame indicates the need to observe the child carefully and systematically. (See the Developmental Alerts at the end of each age profile.)

Sitting, walking, and talking are examples of biological maturation, yet these skills do not develop independently of the environment. Learning to walk, for example, requires muscle strength and coordination. It also requires an environment that encourages practice, not only of walking as it emerges, but also of the behaviors and skills that precede walking, such as rolling over, sitting, and standing.

Sequences of Development

A sequence of development is comprised of predictable steps along a developmental pathway common to the majority of children. Children must be able to roll over before they can sit and sit before they can stand. *The critical consideration is the order in which children acquire these developmental skills, not their age in months and years.* The appropriate sequence in each area of development is an important indication that the child is moving steadily forward along a sound developmental continuum; Figure 1-5. In language development, for example, it does not matter how many words a child speaks by two years of age. What is important is that the child has progressed from cooing and babbling to "jabbering" (inflected **jargon**) to syllable production. The two- or three-year-old who has progressed through these stages usually produces words and sentences within a reasonable period of time.

---

jargon—unintelligible speech; in young children, it usually includes sounds and inflections of the native language.

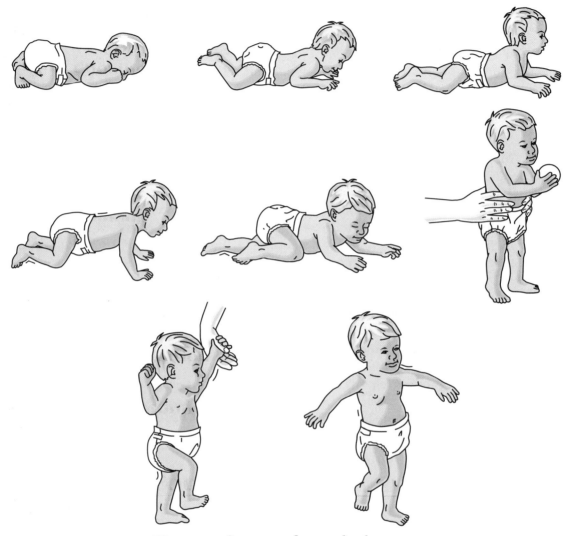

Figure 1-5 Sequence of motor development.

Developmental progress is rarely smooth and even. Irregularities, such as periods of **stammering** or the onset of a **food jag**, may characterize development. Regression, or taking a step or two backward now and then, is perfectly normal: a child who has been toilet trained may begin to have "accidents" when starting preschool or child care.

---

stammering—to speak in an interrupted or repetitive pattern (not to be confused with stuttering).
food jag—a period when only certain foods are preferred or accepted.

Age-Level Expectancies or Norms

Age-level expectancies can be thought of as **chronological** or age-related levels of development. Investigators like Gesell and Piaget carried out hundreds of systematic observations of infants and children of various ages. Analyses of their findings represent the average or typical age at which many specifically described developmental skills are acquired by most children in a given culture. This average age is often called the **norm;** thus a child's development may be described as at the norm, above the norm, or below the norm. For example, a child who walks at eight months is ahead of the norm (twelve to fifteen months), while a child who does not walk until twenty months is below the norm.

Age-level expectancies *always represent a range and never an exact point in time* when specific skills will be achieved. Profiles in this text of age expectancies for specific skills always should be interpreted as approximate midpoints on a range of months (as in the example on walking, from eight to twenty months with the midpoint at fourteen months). Once again, a reminder: it is *sequence* and *not age* that is the important factor in evaluating a child's progress. In real life, there is probably no child who is truly typical in every way. The range of skills and the age at which skills are acquired show great variation. Relevant again is the example of walking, one infant starting at eight months and another not until twenty months (many months apart on either side of the norm). No two children grow and develop at exactly the same rate, nor do they perform in exactly the same way. There are a half dozen ways of creeping and crawling. Most children, however, use what is referred to as *contralateral locomotion,* an opposite knee–hand method of getting about prior to walking. Yet, some normally walking two-year olds never crawl, indicating great variation in typical development.

Organization and Reorganization

Development can be thought of as a series of phases. Spurts of rapid growth and development often are followed by periods of disorganization. Then the child seems to recover and move into a period of reorganization. It is not uncommon for children to demonstrate behavior problems or even regression during these periods; Figure 1-6. The reasons vary. Perhaps a new baby has become an active and engaging older infant who is now the center of family attention. Three-year-old brother may revert to babyish ways about the same time. He begins to have tantrums over minor frustrations and may, for the time being, lose his hard-won bladder control. Usually, these periods are short-lived. The three-year-old, for

---

chronological—events or dates in sequence in the passage of time.
norms—age-level expectancies associated with the achievement of developmental skills.

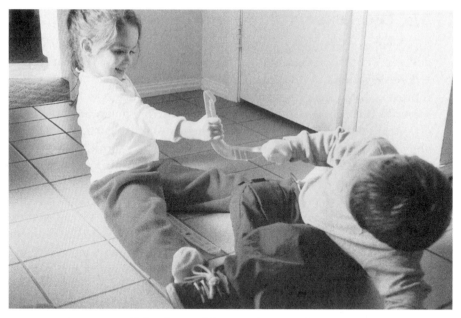

Figure 1-6 Behavior problems and regression are common.

example, will almost always learn more age-appropriate ways of getting attention if given adequate adult support and understanding.

Interrelatedness of Developmental Domains

Discussions about development usually focus on several major domains: physical, motor, perceptual, cognitive, personal-social, and language. However, no single area develops independently of other developmental areas. Every skill, whether simple or complex, is a mixture. Social skills are an example. Why are some young children said to have good social skills? Often the answer is because they play well with other children and are sought out as playmates. To be a preferred playmate, a child must have many skills, all of them interrelated and interdependent. A four-year-old, for example, should be able to:

■ Run, jump, climb, and build with blocks (good motor skills).
■ Ask for, explain, and describe what is going on (good language skills).
■ Recognize likenesses and differences among play materials and so select appropriate materials in a joint building project (good perceptual skills).
■ Problem-solve, conceptualize, and plan ahead in cooperative play ventures (good cognitive skills).

Every developmental area is well represented in the above example, even though social development was the primary area under consideration.

Individual Differences

A number of factors, in addition to genetic and biological ones, contribute to making each child unique, special, different from every other child.

Temperament. Temperament refers to an individual's responses to everyday happenings. Infants and young children differ in their activity levels, alertness, irritability, soothability, restlessness, and willingness to cuddle. Such qualities often lead to labels—the "easy" child, the "difficult" child, the "slow-to-warm" child. These characteristics (and labels) seem to have a definite effect on how family and teachers respond to the child. Their responses, in turn, reinforce the child's self-perceptions. For example, a slow-to-warm child may evoke few displays of affection from others and so perceive this as rejection, making it even more difficult for the child to act warm and outgoing.

Gender Roles. Early in life, young children learn gender roles appropriate to their culture. Each boy and girl develops a set of behaviors, attitudes, and commitments that are defined, directly or indirectly, as acceptable male or female attributes. In addition, each child plays out gender roles according to everyday experiences. The child's sense of maleness or femaleness will be influenced by playmates and play opportunities, toys, type and amount of television viewing, and especially adult models (parents, neighbors, teachers).

Ecological Factors. Starting at conception, ecology—the environmental influence of family and home, community and society—affects all aspects of development. Listed below are examples of powerful ecological factors.

■ Income level; adequacy of food and shelter.
■ General health and nutrition; availability of pre- and postnatal care for mother and child.
■ Parents' education level (mother's level of education is a major predictor of a child's school achievement).
■ Parents' understanding of obligations and responsibilities before and after the infant's birth.
■ Patterns of communication and child rearing practices (loving or punishing, nurturing or neglectful); amount of family stress.
■ Family structure—single- or two-parent, extended family, nontraditional household; foster homes.

Factors such as these contribute to each child being unlike any other child. For example, the child born to a single, fifteen-year-old parent living in poverty will be

---

ecology—in terms of children's development, refers to interactive effects between children and their family, child care situation, school, and everything in the wider community that impacts their lives.

different from a child born and reared in a two-parent, working-class, or professional family.

Transactional Patterns of Development

From birth, the child influences the behavior of parents and caregivers. In turn, parents and caregivers influence the child. Thus, development is a give-and-take process in which parents, caregivers, teachers, and the child are continuously interacting in ways that influence each other's behaviors. For example, a calm, cuddly baby expresses its needs in a clear and predictable fashion. This infant begins life with personal-social experiences that are quite different from those of a tense, colicky infant whose sleeping and eating patterns are highly irregular and often stressful to parents. The transactional process between infants and parents will be quite different in each instance and so will the developmental outcome in all likelihood.

Infants and young children thrive when adults respond promptly and positively, at least a fair share of the time, to appropriate things a child says and does. Research indicates that children develop healthier self-concepts, as well as earlier and better language, cognitive, and social skills when raised by responsive adults.

ATYPICAL DEVELOPMENT

The term *atypical* is used to describe children with developmental differences, deviations, or marked delays: children whose development appears to be incomplete or inconsistent with typical patterns and sequences. The child with developmental delays performs in one or more areas of development like a much younger child. The child who is still babbling with no recognizable words beyond age three is an example of delayed development. This condition need not be disabling unless the child never develops **functional language.** *Developmental deviation* refers to an aspect of development that is different from what is ever seen in typical development. The child born with six toes or with a profound hearing loss has a developmental deviation. The six-toed child is not likely to be disabled. In contrast, the child who is deaf may have a serious and lifelong disability without early and intensive intervention. In any event, the concepts and principles described in the foregoing pages apply to the child with developmental differences as well as the child who is said to be developing typically. It must be remembered that a child with any kind of a developmental problem is first of all a child with the same basic needs as all other children. The principles outlined in this chapter

---

functional language—*language that allows children to get what they need or want.*

provide the foundation for quality **inclusion programs** for all young children, regardless of their capabilities and backgrounds.

 ## SUMMARY

Today's knowledge of child development is a composite of four traditional psychological approaches to human development: maturational, psychoanalytic, cognitive/developmental, and learning theory. All theories agree that meeting the essential physical and psychological needs of infants and children is a powerful determinant of optimum development. Paramount among these needs are adequate physical care, responsive nurturing, and abundant opportunities to learn and develop self-esteem.

Over the years, age-level expectancies (norms) have been used to assess children's progress in all of the developmental domains. The range of normalcy is broad; typical development shows great variability, and each child is unique. In assessing developmental progress it is the sequential acquisition of basic skills that is significant, not the child's age per se. Atypical development is usually characterized by marked delays or characteristics never seen in typical development. Nevertheless, it must be remembered that atypical children have the same essential needs as all other children.

 ## KEY TERMS

at-risk	jargon
chronological	nature/nurture
cumulative	neurological
descriptive praise	normal (typical) development
developmentally appropriate	norms
ecology	nurturing
essential needs	reciprocal
food jag	self-esteem
functional language	stammering
inclusion programs	

---

inclusion programs—community child care, school, and recreational facilities in which all children from the most gifted to the most disabled participate in the same activities. Inclusion is a federal law mandated by the Congress of the United States. Originally it was referred to as mainstreaming.

APPLY YOUR KNOWLEDGE

A. Apply What You Have Learned

Reread the developmental sketch about Joel at the beginning of the chapter. How might you answer the following questions?

1. As foster parents, which essential physical needs are Berta and Doug presumably providing for Joel?

2. What are some of Joel's fundamental psychological needs and how are his foster parents attempting to meet them?

3. Could Joel's early months of living in an impoverished environment have any effect on his current development? Explain.

4. Although Joel's motor skill development may be delayed, he has learned to sit up, crawl, stand, walk, and eventually run. Which is most important to consider in his case—the fact that he was older than is typical when he learned these skills, or that he has developed them in this particular order? Explain.

5. Based on the brief description of Joel and his family, what reciprocal effect might you anticipate will occur when Joel crawls up onto his father's lap?

B. Review Questions

1. List four major developmental theories and give an identifying characteristic of each.

2. List three psychological needs of the developing child.

3. List three physical needs of the developing child.

4. List three ways in which an adult can show respect for a young child's accomplishments.

5. List three ecological factors that influence early development.

 ## HELPFUL WEB SITES

Children, Youth & Families Education
    & Research Network   http://www.cyfernet.org

Council for Exceptional Children   http://www.cec.sped.org

I Am Your Child	http://www.iamyourchild.org
National Institute of Child Health & Human Development	http://www.nichd.nih.gov
National Academy for Child Development	http://www.nacd.org
Society for Research in Child Development	http://www.srcd.org

For additional child development resources, visit our Web site www.earlychilded.delmar.com

Growth and Development

 ## OBJECTIVES

After reading this chapter, you should be able to:

- Define growth and development as separate concepts and give at least two examples of each.
- Identify the six major developmental domains that are the focus of this text.
- Describe the role of the environment in early brain development.
- Explain the importance of using sequences of development rather than chronological age in assessing developmental progress.
- Discuss what is meant when an infant or child is said to be at-risk, listing at least five factors that lead to high-risk early development.

MEET THE TWINS, AMY AND BART

The twins, Amy and Bart, soon to be three years old, weighed in at a little over five pounds each at birth and have remained strong and healthy. They look much alike, with dark brown eyes, thick eyelashes, and high cheekbones. Although they behave alike in many ways, there are marked differences. Since early infancy, Amy has been more physically active. She slept less, ate more, sat up, crawled, and walked alone weeks before Bart or other babies her age. She also has been more adventuresome in trying out new experiences such as slides and climbing equipment. Bart, on the other hand, was the first to smile, play peek-a-boo, and say recognizable words. He now uses complete sentences and has considerable letter, word, and number recognition skills. He likes to "read" to Amy and also acts as her interpreter when she can't make herself understood. In turn, Amy is first to comfort Bart when he is hurt or frightened. Recently, the two were enrolled in a child care program where they adjusted easily but still stay close to each other throughout the day.

BASIC PATTERNS AND CONCEPTS

Groups of children of approximately the same age appear to be remarkably similar in size, shape, and abilities. Closer observation, however, reveals a wide range of individual differences. Both similarities and differences depend on a child's unique patterns of growth and development. What defines this complementary process, *growth and development*? Although the terms tend to be used interchangeably, they are not identical concepts.

Growth. **Growth** refers to specific physical changes and increases in the child's actual size; Figure 2-1. Additional numbers of cells, as well as enlargement of existing cells, account for the observable increases in a child's height, weight, **head circumference,** shoe size, length of arms and legs, and body shape. All growth changes lend themselves to direct and fairly reliable measurement.

The growth process continues through much of the life span; but, the rate of growth varies according to age. For example, growth occurs rapidly during infancy and adolescence and is slower and less dramatic in the school-age child. Even into old age, although much less vigorously, the body continues to repair and re-place its cells.

Development. **Development** refers to an increase in complexity—a change from the relatively simple to the more complicated and detailed. The process involves an orderly progression along a continuum or pathway. Little by little, knowledge, behaviors, and skills become increasingly more refined and expanded. The sequence is basically the same for all children. However, the rate of develop-ment shows great variability from child to child (see Chapter 1).

Rate and level of development are closely related to physiological maturity of the nervous, muscular, and skeletal systems. Also, development is influenced by heredity and environmental factors unique to each individual; these account for the wide range of variations in individual children.

---

growth—*physical changes leading to an increase in size.*
head circumference—*measurement of the head taken at its largest point (across the forehead, around the back of head, returning to the starting point).*
development—*refers to an increase in complexity, from simple to more complicated and detailed.*

Figure 2-1 Growth is an increase in size.

Brain Growth and Development. The maturing of the brain lays the foundation for all other aspects of a child's development. Head circumference is an important physical measurement that should be taken regularly in young infants and children because it provides information about the growth of the brain. In the fetus, brain development is rapid, exceedingly complex, and largely determined by genetic mechanisms. Recent research indicates that changes in the brain's composition are related to experience. Early on, there are many more brain cells (neurons) than the child will need, and connections between cells continue to form. This results in necessary and natural *pruning*, which allows active cells and connections to be strengthened and those that are unused to drop away. This explains, for example, why the *lazy eye* in a child with **strabismus** will eventually become blind unless there is early, specialized intervention. Thus, both genetic factors and experience are significant in brain growth and development.

Current research also reveals amazing information about the relationship between the brain and language development. For example, infants not only take

---

strabismus—condition in which one or both eyes appear to be turned inward (crossed) or outward.

in the sounds of the language they are hearing, but they replicate them, complete with a dialect, if one is present, in family and caregiving situations. Furthermore, the dialect is maintained without change for years to come. It's as if, in the case of language development, the brain will not easily sever connections made in the earliest months and years of life, regardless of subsequent changes in language environments. Other findings from recent brain research will be discussed throughout the text as they relate to particular aspects of development.

Typical Growth and Development. This is a term used to indicate **acquisition** of certain skills and behaviors according to a predictable rate and sequence. As noted in Chapter 1, the range of what is considered normal is broad. It includes mild variations and simple irregularities, such as the three-year-old who lisps or the twelve-month-old who learns to walk without having crawled.

At-risk. Infants and young children who seem likely to develop physical problems, learning disabilities, or behavior difficulties are described as being *at-risk*. Low birth weight is a common contributing factor. It can be caused by poor maternal health, inadequate medical care or substance abuse during pregnancy, and maternal age outside the "normal" range (very young teenagers and women in their middle forties and older). Children who experience abuse or neglect tend also to be at high risk.

Atypical. This term is used to describe a child whose growth or development is inconsistent with expectations of what is viewed as normal or typical. Abnormal development in one area may or may not interfere with development in other areas. There are many causes of atypical development, including genetic errors, poor health and nutrition, injury, and too few opportunities to learn.

DEVELOPMENTAL DOMAINS

To describe and accurately assess children's progress, a developmental framework is needed. In this book we focus on six major developmental areas, or domains: physical, motor, perceptual, cognitive, speech and language, and personal-social. Each domain includes the many kinds of skills and behaviors that will be discussed in the developmental profiles which are the major focus of this book (Chapters 4 through 8). Although these developmental areas are separated for the purpose of discussion, they cannot be separated from one another in reality. Each is integrally related to, and **interdependent** with, each of the others in the overall developmental process.

---

acquisition—the process of learning or achieving objectives (walking, counting, reading).
interdependent—affecting or influencing development in other domains.

Developmental profiles or "word pictures" are useful for assessing both the immediate and ongoing status of children's skills and behavior. It is important to keep in mind that the rate of development is uneven and occasionally unpredictable across areas. For example, the language and social skills of infants and toddlers typically are less well developed than their ability to move about. Also, children's individual achievements may vary across developmental areas: a child may walk late, but talk early. Again, an important reminder: development in any of the domains is dependent in large part on children having appropriate stimulation and adequately supported opportunities to learn.

Physical Development and Growth. This domain governs the major tasks of infancy and childhood. Understanding the patterns and sequences of physical development is essential to being effective parents, teachers, and caregivers. It is healthy growth and development, not adult pressure or coaching, that makes new learnings and behaviors possible. Adult pressure cannot hurry the process and in fact is more likely to be counterproductive. A seven-month-old infant cannot be toilet trained; the **sphincter** muscles are not yet developed enough to exert such control. Nor can the majority of kindergartners catch or kick a ball skillfully; such coordination is impossible given a five- or six-year-old's stage of physical development, yet most of us have seen a Pee Wee League coach or parent reduce a child to tears for missing a catch or a kick.

Governed by heredity and greatly influenced by environmental conditions, physical development and growth is a highly individualized process. It is responsible for changes in body shape and proportions as well as overall body size. Growth, especially that of the brain, occurs more rapidly during prenatal development and the first year than at any other time. Growth is intricately related to progress in other developmental areas. It is responsible for increasing muscle strength for movement, for coordinating vision and motor control, and for synchronizing neurological and muscular activity in gaining bladder and bowel control. The state of a child's physical development serves as a reliable index of general health and well-being. It also has a direct influence on determining whether children are likely to achieve their potential in cognitive development and academic achievement.

Motor Development. The child's ability to move about and control the various body parts is the major function of this domain. Refinements in motor development depend on maturation of the brain, input from the *sensory system,* increased bulk and number of muscle fibers, a healthy nervous system, and opportunities to practice. This holistic approach contrasts markedly with the way early developmentalists saw the emergence of motor skills. They described a purely maturational process, governed almost entirely by instructions on the individual's

---

sphincter—the muscles necessary to accomplish bowel and bladder control.

genetic code. Today's psychologists consider such an explanation misleading and incomplete. Their research indicates that when young children show an interest, for example, in using a spoon to feed themselves, it is always accompanied by improved eye–hand coordination (to direct the spoon to the mouth), motivation (*liking* and *wanting* to eat what is in the bowl), and the drive to imitate what others are doing. In other words, the environment, that is, experience, plays a major role in the emergence of new motor skills.

Motor activity during very early infancy is purely **reflexive** and disappears as the child develops **voluntary** control. If these earliest reflexes do not phase out at appropriate times in the **developmental sequence**, it may be an indication of neurological problems (see Appendix 1). In such cases, medical evaluation should be sought.

Three principles govern motor development:

1. **Cephalocaudal:** bone and muscular development that proceeds from head to toe; Figure 2-2. The infant first learns to control muscles that support the head and neck, then the trunk, and later those that allow reaching. Muscles for walking develop last.
2. **Proximodistal:** bone and muscular development that begins with improved control of muscles closest to the central portion of the body, gradually moving outward and away from the midpoint to the extremities (arms and legs); Figure 2-3. Control of the head and neck is achieved before the child can pick up an object with thumb and forefinger (pincer grasp or finger–thumb opposition).
3. **Refinement:** muscular development that progresses from the general to the specific in both **gross motor** and **fine motor** activities; Figure 2-4. In the refinement of a gross motor skill, for example, a two-year-old may attempt to throw a ball but achieves little distance or control. The same child, within a few short years, may pitch a ball over home plate with speed and accuracy.

---

reflexive—movements resulting from impulses of the nervous system that cannot be controlled by the individual.

voluntary—movements that can be willed and purposively controlled and initiated by the individual.

developmental sequence—a continuum of predictable steps along a developmental pathway of skill achievement.

cephalocaudal—bone and muscular development that proceeds from head to toe.

proximodistal—bone and muscular development that begins closest to the trunk, gradually moving outward to the extremities.

refinement—progressive improvement in ability to perform fine and gross motor skills.

gross motor—large muscle movements, such as locomotor skills (walking, skipping, swimming) and nonlocomotive movements (sitting, pushing and pulling, squatting).

fine motor skills—also referred to as manipulative skills; includes stacking blocks, buttoning and zipping, and toothbrushing.

Figure 2-2 Cephalocaudal development proceeds from head to toe.

Figure 2-3 Proximodistal development proceeds outward from the trunk.

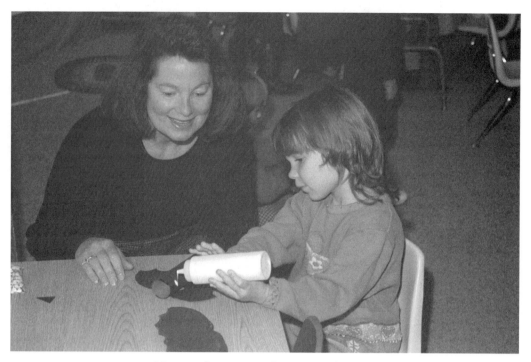

Figure 2-4 Motor refinement refers to the fine-tuning of a skill.

As for a fine motor skill, compare the self-feeding efforts of a toddler with an eight-year-old who is motivated (for whatever reason) to display good table manners!

Perceptual Development. This is the increasingly complex way the child makes use of information received through the senses: sight, hearing, touch, smell, taste, and body position. It might be said that perception is a significant factor that determines and orchestrates the functioning of the various senses, singly or in combination. The perceptual process also enables the individual to focus on what is relevant at a particular moment and to screen out whatever is irrelevant. In other words: Which details are important? Which differences should be noted? Which should be ignored?

Three aspects of perceptual development will be addressed:

1. **Multisensory:** Information is generally received through more than one sense organ at a time. When listening to a speaker, we use sight (watching facial expressions and gestures) and sound (listening to the words).

multisensory—information received through more than one sense organ at a time.

Figure 2-5 Habituation involves the ability to concentrate on a task.

2. *Habituation:* This is the ability to ignore everything except what is most important to the immediate situation; Figure 2-5. Example: the child who is unaware of a conversation in the background and focuses, instead, on his book.
3. *Sensory integration:* This process involves the translation of **sensory information** into functional behavior; the five-year-old sees a car coming and waits for it to pass; Figure 2-6.

The basic perceptual system is in place at birth. Through experience, learning, and maturation it develops into a smoothly coordinated operation for processing complex information. Because of this mechanism, children can sort shapes according to size and color and make fine discriminations: hearing the difference among initial sounds in rhyming words, such as rake, cake, lake. The sensory system also enables each of us to respond appropriately to all kinds of messages and signals, such as smiling in response to a smile or keeping quiet in response to a frown.

Cognitive Development. This has to do with the expansion of a child's intellect or mental abilities. Cognition involves recognizing, processing, and organizing

---

sensory information—*information received through the senses: eyes, ears, nose, mouth, touch.*

Figure 2-6 Sensory integration involves translating what is seen and heard into behavior.

information and then using the information appropriately. The cognitive process includes such mental activities as discovering, interpreting, sorting, classifying, and remembering. In older children it means evaluating ideas, making judgments, solving problems, understanding rules and concepts, thinking ahead, and visualizing possibilities or consequences. Cognitive development is an ongoing process of interaction between the child and his or her perceptual view of objects or events in the environment. It is probably safe to say that neither cognitive nor perceptual development can proceed independently of the other.

The development of cognition begins with the primitive or reflexive behaviors that support survival and early learning in the healthy newborn. One example of very early learning: when a mother playfully sticks out her tongue several times and the baby begins to imitate her. This, and other early behaviors, led developmental psychologists to ponder the many striking similarities in how infants and children learn. Based on repeated observations of such similarities, the Swiss psychologist, Jean Piaget, in the 1950s formulated four stages in cognitive development:

Sensorimotor (approximately birth to two years): Reflexive behavior gives way to intentional behavior. Example: the child sees an object and reaches for it.
Preoperational (approximately two to seven years): Children begin thinking in symbols about things in their immediate environment. Example: the three-

year-old picks up a long stick and calls it a fishing pole. This example also shows a second aspect of the preoperational stage, the emergence of language, which is another form of symbol usage.

Concrete operations (begins between five and seven years): Children now are in the process of developing internal schemes for understanding their immediate world. These emerging *schema* (Piaget's term) lead to understanding such things as basic math and spatial concepts.

Formal operations (beginning at about twelve and continuing to develop into early adulthood) During these years the teenager develops complex thinking skills related not only to objects and experiences, but also to abstract thoughts and ideas.

Cognitive skills always overlap with both perceptual development and motor involvement and starting early in the second year, comes another overlap, the emergence of speech and language.

Language Development. Language is often defined as a system of symbols, spoken, written, and gestural (waving, scowling, cowering) that allows us to communicate with one another. Normal language development is regular and sequential and depends on maturation as well as learning opportunities. The first year of life is called the prelinguistic or prelanguage phase. The child is totally dependent on body movements and sounds such as crying and laughing to convey needs and feelings. This is followed during the second year by the linguistic or language stage, in which speech becomes the major way of communicating. Over the next three or four years, the child learns to put words together to form simple and then compound sentences that make sense because the child has learned the appropriate grammatical constructions. Between five and seven years of age, most children have become skilled at conveying their thoughts and ideas verbally. Many children at this age have a vocabulary of 14,000 words or more, which may double or triple during middle childhood, depending on a child's language environment.

Most children seem to understand a variety of concepts and relationships long before they have the words to describe them. This is referred to as *receptive language,* which precedes *expressive language* (the ability to speak words to describe and explain). Speech and language development is closely related to the child's general cognitive, social, perceptual, and neuromuscular development. Language development also depends greatly on the type of language the child hears in the family and in the community.

Personal and Social Development. This is a broad area that covers how children feel about themselves and their relationships with others. It refers to children's behaviors and responses to play and work activities, attachments to parents and caregivers, and relationships with brothers, sisters, and friends. Gender roles, independence, morality, trust, and accepting rules and laws are also basic aspects of personal and social development. The family and its cultural values are major influences in shaping a child's social development and basic personality traits.

In describing personal and social development, it must be remembered that children develop at different rates. Individual differences in genetic and cultural background, health status, and such factors as experiences in child care, contribute to these variations. No two children can ever be exactly alike, not in personal social development or in any other area of development.

 ## AGE DIVISIONS

The age divisions listed below and used throughout this book are commonly referred to by many child developmentalists when describing significant changes within developmental areas:

Infancy	birth to one month
	1–4 months
	4–8 months
	8–12 months
Toddlerhood	12–24 months
	24–36 months
Early Childhood	3–5 years
	6–8 years
Middle Childhood	9–12 years

Age divisions are to be used with extreme caution and great flexibility when dealing with real children. They are based on the averaged achievements, abilities, and behaviors of large numbers of children at various stages in development. As stated again and again, there is great variation from one child to another. It is the sequential acquisition of developmental tasks, *not age,* that is the major index to healthy development.

The step-by-step development that we detail in Chapters 4 through 8 speaks to the importance of understanding that it is sequence and not age that indicates developmental progress in each domain and in the overall development of each child.

 ## SUMMARY

Growth and development are influenced by a child's unique genetic makeup and the quality of the everyday environment, which includes nurturing, health care, and opportunities to learn the vast range of skills that give evidence of developmental progress. Each child's well-being depends on acquiring the necessary skills in six developmental domains: physical, motor, perceptual, cognitive, language, and personal-social. Although the six domains are separated for discussion purposes, they are interwoven and interdependent during the developmental years and throughout life.

While age-level expectations (*norms*) are of some value in assessing an individual child's developmental status, the more important factor is not age but sequence: Is the child going through each step in each area of development even though it may be somewhat later (or earlier) than most children of similar age?

 ## KEY TERMS

acquisition	interdependent
cephalocaudal	multisensory
development	proximodistal
developmental sequence	reflexive
fine motor	sensory information
gross motor	sphincter
growth	strabismus
head circumference	voluntary

APPLY YOUR KNOWLEDGE

A. Apply What You Have Learned

Reread the brief developmental sketch about Amy and Bart at the beginning of the chapter. How might you answer the following questions?

1. From the brief descriptions of Amy and Bart, which characteristics could be attributed solely to genetic makeup?

2. In what ways do Amy's and Bart's motor skill development differ?

3. What is "refinement"? Give an example of this developmental principle from the descriptions of Amy and Bart.

4. How do Amy and Bart differ in terms of their personal-social development? Given that they are twins, what factors might account for these differences?

5. According to Piaget, which stage of cognitive development are the twins, who are almost three, currently experiencing? Give an example of this concept from the descriptions of Amy and Bart.

6. Just because Amy and Bart are twins, should you expect them to grow and develop in exactly the same way and at exactly the same rate? Explain.

B. Review Questions

1. List three factors that influence a child's rate of development.

2. List three factors that may lead to atypical development.

3. List three sources of perceptual information.

4. List Piaget's four stages of cognitive development with approximate ages.

5. List three factors that can put an infant at high risk developmentally.

 HELPFUL WEB SITES

Developmentally Appropriate Practices in Early Childhood Programs Serving Children Birth Through Age 8	http://www.newhorizons.org/NAEYC
Educational Resources Information Center (ERIC)	http://www.eric.ed.gov
Indian Health Service	http://www.ihs.gov
National Black Child Development Institute	http://www.nbcdi.org
National Center for Early Development & Learning Center (ERIC)	http://www.fpg.unc.edu/~ncedl/
National Institute on Early Childhood Development & Education (U.S. Department of Education)	http://www.ed.gov/offices/OERI/ECI

 For additional child development resources, visit our Web site www.earlychilded.delmar.com

Chapter 3

Prenatal Development

 OBJECTIVES

After reading this chapter, you should be able to:
- Describe how implantation exposes the embryo to environmental risks.
- Discuss the functional roles of the placenta.
- Explain why medical supervision is important during pregnancy.
- Identify nutrients that are required in greater amounts during pregnancy.
- Discuss how a mother's age influences fetal development.
- List five teratogens.

MEET ANNA AND MIGUEL

Anna and Miguel were elated when they learned she was seven weeks' pregnant. Six months earlier, Anna had experienced a miscarriage during her third month of pregnancy. At the time, Anna's doctor advised her to stop smoking before attempting future pregnancies. Although she wasn't able to quit, she did significantly reduce the number of cigarettes she was smoking each day. Anna also made an effort to improve her diet by eating more fruits and vegetables and eliminating alcohol consumption.

When Anna and Miguel shared their exciting news with family members, everyone had advice for preventing another miscarriage. Her mother insisted that Anna rest and avoid any type of activity, including cleaning the house and cooking. Miguel's aunt advised Anna not to drink milk and to eat all that she could "because she was now eating for two." Her sister discouraged Anna from continuing her job at the bank, but it was the only way she and Miguel could maintain their health insurance coverage. Anna appreciated their suggestions, but was convinced that everything would be okay this time around.

Each of the approximately 266 days of prenatal development (from **conception** to birth) is critical to producing a healthy newborn. **Genes** inherited from the baby's biological mother and father determine all physical characteristics and, perhaps, **temperament,** as well as any abnormalities. However, because it is the mother who provides everything physically essential (as well as harmful) to the growing fetus, she plays a major role in promoting its healthy development. Her own health and nutritional status, both before and during pregnancy, strongly influence the birth of a healthy baby. When the father provides caring support for the mother throughout the pregnancy, their unborn infant's development may be enhanced. Therefore, it is important that patterns of normal prenatal development, as well as practices that both facilitate and interfere with this process, are clearly understood by every potential parent.

THE DEVELOPMENT PROCESS

The prenatal period is commonly divided into stages. In obstetrical practice, pregnancy is classified according to trimesters, each consisting of three calendar months:

- first trimester—conception through the third month
- second trimester—fourth through the sixth month
- third trimester—seventh through the ninth month

Pregnancy also may be discussed in terms of fetal development. This approach emphasizes critical changes that occur week by week and also encompasses three stages:

- germinal
- embryonic
- fetal

The *germinal stage* refers to the first fourteen days of pregnancy. The union of an ovum and sperm produces a zygote. Soon afterward, cell division begins, gradually

---

conception—the joining of a single egg or ovum from the female and a single sperm from the male.
genes—genetic material that carries codes, or information, for all inherited characteristics.
temperament—an individual's characteristic manner or style of response to everyday events, including degree of interest, activity level, and regulation of own behavior.

forming a pinhead-size mass of specialized cells called a blastocyst. Around the fourteenth day, this small mass attaches itself to the wall of the mother's uterus. Successful attachment (**implantation**) marks the beginning of the **embryo** and the embryonic stage.

The *embryonic stage* includes the third through eighth week of a pregnancy. This stage is critical to the overall development of the fetus. Continuing cell divisions result in specialized cell layers that gradually form major organs and systems, such as the heart, lungs, and brain. Many of these structures will be functional near the end of this period. Embryonic blood, for example, begins to flow through the fetus's primitive cardiovascular system (heart and blood vessels) in the fourth to the fifth weeks.

During this time, other important changes are taking place. Once implantation is completed, a **placenta** begins to form. It serves four major functions:

- to supply nutrients and hormones to the fetus
- to remove fetal waste products throughout the pregnancy
- to filter out many harmful substances, as well as viruses and other disease-causing organisms (Unfortunately, many drugs can get through the placenta's filtering system.)
- to act as a temporary immune system by supplying the fetus with the same antibodies the mother produces against certain infectious diseases (In most instances, the infant is protected for approximately six months following birth.)

An umbilical cord, containing two arteries and one vein, develops as the placenta is forming. This cord establishes a linkage between the fetus and the mother. At this point, the fetus is affected by the mother's general health and lifestyle and is highly vulnerable when exposed to certain chemical substances, such as alcohol and certain medications (see Table 3-2) or infectious illnesses (see Table 3-3) that may enter her body. Exposure to these substances can seriously damage the major fetal organs and systems that are developing during these critical periods of early pregnancy. As we will see in a later section, the result may be irreversible birth defects, ranging from mild to severe.

The *fetal stage* refers to the period between the ninth week and the end of pregnancy or onset of labor and delivery (around the thirty-eighth week). Most systems and structures are now formed and so, this final and longest period is devoted to growth and maturity; Table 3-1. During the final two months, few developmental changes occur. Instead, there are rapid and important gains in weight and size; a

---

implantation—*the attachment of the blastocyst to the wall of the mother's uterus; occurs around the twelfth day.*
embryo—*the cell mass from the time of implantation through the eighth week of pregnancy.*
placenta—*a specialized lining that forms inside the uterus during pregnancy to support and nourish the developing fetus.*

Table 3-1 Characteristics of Fetal Development

2 weeks	■ Cell division results in an embryo consisting of sixteen cells.
3–8 weeks	■ Structures necessary to support the developing embryo have formed: placenta, chorionic sac, amniotic fluid, and umbilical cord. ■ Embryonic cell layers begin to specialize, developing into major internal organs and systems, as well as external structures. ■ First bone cells appear. ■ Less than one inch (2.54 cm) in length at eight weeks.
12 weeks	■ Weighs approximately 1 to 2 ounces (0.029–0.006 kg) and is nearly 3 inches (7.6 cm) in length. ■ Sex organs develop; baby's gender can be determined. ■ Kidneys begin to function. ■ Arms, legs, fingers, and toes are well defined and movable. ■ Forms facial expressions (e.g., smiling, looking around), and is able to suck and swallow.
16 weeks	■ Weighs about 5 ounces (0.14 kg) and is 6 inches (15.2 cm) in length. ■ Sucks thumb. ■ Moves about actively; mother may begin to feel baby's movement (called "quickening"). ■ Has strong heartbeat that can be heard.
20 weeks	■ Weighs nearly one pound (0.46 kg) and has grown to approximately 11 to 12 inches (27.9–30.5 cm) in length (approximately half of baby's birth length). ■ Experiences occasional hiccups. ■ Eyelashes, eyebrows, and hair forming; eyes remain closed.
24 weeks	■ Weight doubles to about 1.5 to 2 pounds (0.68–0.90 kg) and length increases to 12 to 14 inches (30.5–35.6 cm). ■ Eyes are well formed, often open; responds to light and sound. ■ Grasp reflex develops. ■ Skin is wrinkled, thin, and covered with a covering of soft hair called *lanugo* and a white, greasy, protective substance called *vernix caseosa*.
28 weeks	■ Weighs about 3 to 3.5 pounds (1.4–1.6 kg); grows to approximately 16 to 17 inches (40.6–43 cm) in length. ■ Develops a sleep/wake pattern. ■ Remains very active; kicks and pokes mother's ribs and abdomen. ■ Able to survive if born prematurely, although lungs are not yet fully developed.
32 weeks	■ Weighs approximately 5 to 6 pounds (2.3–2.7 kg) and is 17 to 18 inches in length (43–45.7 cm). ■ Baby takes iron and calcium from mother's diet to build up reserve stores. ■ Becomes less active due to larger size and less room for moving about.
36–38 weeks	■ Weighs an average of 7 to 8 pounds (3.2–3.6 kg) at birth; length is approximately 19 to 21 inches (48–53.3 cm). ■ Moves into final position (usually head down) in preparation for birth. ■ Loses most of lanugo (body hair); skin still somewhat wrinkled and red. ■ Is much less active (has little room in which to move). ■ Body systems are more mature (especially the lungs and heart), thus increasing baby's chances of survival at birth.

seven-month-old fetus weighs 2 to 3 pounds (0.9–1.4 kg) and will gain approximately 1/2 pound (0.23 kg) per week until birth. Body systems also are maturing and growing stronger, improving the fetus's chances of surviving outside the mother's body.

PROMOTING OPTIMUM FETAL DEVELOPMENT

Critical aspects of development are taking place during the earliest days of pregnancy, often before pregnancy has even been confirmed. Therefore, it is important that both mother and father practice healthy lifestyles throughout their reproductive years. Current research provides essential information about many factors that can improve a mother's chances of having a healthy baby, including:

- professional prenatal care
- good nutrition
- sufficient rest
- moderate weight gain
- regular exercise
- positive emotional state
- mother's age and general health
- avoidance of drugs, alcohol, and tobacco

Prenatal Care

Medically supervised prenatal care is critical for ensuring the development of a healthy baby; Figure 3-1. Arrangements for such care should be made as soon as a woman suspects that she is pregnant. Women should not rely solely on home pregnancy tests before seeking medical care because the results are not always accurate, especially during the early days and weeks of pregnancy. During the initial visit to a health care provider, pregnancy can be confirmed (or refuted), and any medical problems the mother may have can be evaluated and treated. Counseling on practices that influence fetal development will also be provided. For example, mothers may be encouraged to participate in a program of regular non-contact exercise. (As long as there are no complications, regular exercise can improve weight control, circulation, muscle tone, and elimination, and is believed to contribute to an easier labor and delivery.)

Nutrition

A mother's nutritional status, determined by what she eats before and during pregnancy, has a significant effect on her own health, as well as on that of the

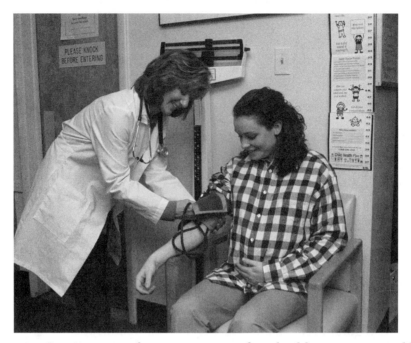

Figure 3-1 Routine prenatal care is important for a healthy pregnancy and baby.

developing fetus; Figure 3-2. Good maternal nutrition lessens the risk of having a low birth weight or premature baby, two conditions often associated with serious developmental problems.

It is important that pregnant women continue to follow the Food Guide Pyramid recommendations to ensure an adequate intake of essential nutrients and calories (www.nal.usda.gov/fnic/Fpyr/pyramid.html); Figure 3-3. In addition, pregnancy increases a woman's dietary need for calories (energy), proteins, fluids, and certain vitamins, such as folacin (folate), B-6, B-12, C, and D, and minerals, such as iron and calcium. Recent findings, for example, have linked adequate folacin intake before and during pregnancy (400 micrograms for nonpregnant women, 600 micrograms daily for pregnant women) with a reduced incidence of spina bifida (a malformation of the baby's spinal column). Folacin (folate) is a B vitamin found in many foods, especially raw leafy green vegetables, dried beans, lentils, orange juice, and fortified pastas, breads, and breakfast cereals. Breastfeeding further increases a mother's need for these nutrients and calories.

While vitamin supplements are generally prescribed, they must not be considered a substitute for a nutritious diet. They lack essential proteins, calories, and other important nutrients found in foods that are required for healthy fetal devel-

Figure 3-2 Good nutrition is essential during pregnancy.

opment and aid the body in fully utilizing vitamins and minerals provided in tablet form. Herbal preparations are not recommended due to a lack of sufficient information about their safety during pregnancy.

Weight

What is the optimum weight gain during pregnancy? This question has been debated for decades. Today, most medical practitioners agree that a woman should ideally gain between 25 and 30 pounds (10–11.4 kg) over the nine-month period. Gains considerably under or over this range can pose increased risks for both the mother and child during pregnancy and at birth.

Following a diet that is nutritionally adequate helps ensure optimum weight gain. Including adequate servings of a wide variety of fruits and vegetables also assures that vitamins critical for fetal growth (vitamins A, C) and fiber to decrease constipation are supplied. Choosing low-fat dairy products and lean meats and

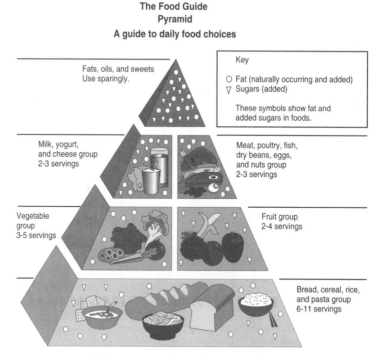

Figure 3-3 Following Food Guide Pyramid recommendations helps assure good nutrition during pregnancy.

plant proteins (e.g., dried beans, legumes, grains) can be helpful for moderating caloric intake while providing key minerals (e.g., iron, calcium) required for the baby's and mother's health throughout the pregnancy. Consuming too many "empty" calories, such as those in junk foods, sweets, and alcohol, can lead to excessive weight gain and also deprive both mother and fetus of critical nutrients found in a well-balanced diet.

Rest and Stress

Pregnancy places significant strains on the mother's body and often increases her sense of fatigue. Additional sleep and occasional periods of rest may help ease these problems. Pregnancy also may induce or increase emotional stress. Prolonged or excessive stress can adversely affect the mother's health, contributing to sleep and eating disorders, high blood pressure, depression, headaches, lowered resistance to infections, and backaches. It can also have harmful effects on the fetus by reducing breathing rate, heart beat, and activity level. While it may not be possible for a pregnant woman to avoid all stress, strain, and fatigue, the ill effects can be lessened with proper rest, nutrition, and exercise.

Age and General Health

A woman's age at the time of conception is an important factor in fetal development. Numerous studies conclude that the early twenties to early thirties are the optimum years for childbearing. The rate of death and developmental disability among babies born to teenage mothers is nearly double that of babies born to women in their twenties. The immaturity of a teenager's reproductive system also increases the risk of giving birth to a premature or low birth weight baby. In addition, teen mothers are more likely to lack access to prenatal care, adequate nourishment and housing, and even basic understanding about how to best care for their own personal needs.

Pregnancy in older women (late thirties and beyond) presents other concerns. Genetic material contained in the ova gradually deteriorates as a woman ages, thus increasing the probability of certain birth defects, such as Down syndrome. New studies also suggest the quality of a male's sperm may lessen with age and exposure to environmental hazards, thus increasing the risk of transmitting damaged chromosomes that can cause birth defects. Older women also tend to experience a higher incidence of medical problems during pregnancy. However, greater awareness of good nutrition, exercise, and medical supervision can improve a mother's chances of having a healthy baby.

Increased knowledge and improved technology are also contributing to a reduction in fetal risk for mothers of all ages. Better genetic counseling, ultrasound scanning (**sonogram**), **CVS, amniocentesis,** and new maternal blood tests allow medical personnel to closely monitor fetal growth and detect specific developmental problems earlier. These procedures are especially useful for many women who are electing to delay childbearing until their late thirties and early forties.

While the risks of pregnancy are undeniably greater for older women and teenagers, the problems often have as much to do with lack of knowledge and poverty as with age. (Exceptions are the chromosomal abnormalities such as Down syndrome.)

---

sonogram—*visual image of the developing fetus created by directing high-frequency soundwaves (ultrasound) at the mother's uterus; used to determine fetal age and physical abnormalities.*

CVS—*Chorionic Villus Sampling; a genetic screening procedure in which a needle is inserted and cells removed from the outer layer of the placenta; performed between the eighth and twelfth weeks to detect some genetic disorders, such as Down syndrome.*

amniocentesis—*genetic screening procedure in which a needle is inserted through the mother's abdomen into the sac of fluids surrounding the fetus to detect abnormalities, such as Down syndrome or spina bifida; usually performed between the twelfth and sixteenth weeks.*

Vast numbers of fetal problems, regardless of maternal age, are closely associated with lack of medical care, poor nutrition, substandard housing, substance abuse, and limited education, all often closely associated with poverty.

THREATS TO OPTIMUM FETAL DEVELOPMENT

While much is known about how to have a healthy baby, there is also much known about the substances and maternal practices that lower those odds. Factors that have negative effects on the developing fetus are known as **teratogens.** Some are especially damaging during the earliest weeks, often before a woman realizes that she is pregnant. It is during these sensitive or critical periods that various fetal structures and major organ systems are rapidly forming and, thus, are most vulnerable to the effects of any harmful substance. The length of these critical periods varies: for example, heart—third to sixth weeks, palate—sixth to eighth weeks. A number of teratogens have been identified through extensive research including:

■ alcohol consumption
■ maternal smoking
■ addictive drugs (e.g., cocaine, heroin, amphetamines)
■ hazardous chemicals (e.g., mercury, lead, carbon monoxide, polychlorinated biphenols [PCBs]), paint solvents
■ some medications; Table 3-2
■ maternal infections; Table 3-3
■ radiation

Researchers also are examining several controversial issues to determine whether there is any possible link to birth defects. Some of these include:

■ prolonged exposure to high temperatures (hot baths, saunas, hot tubs)
■ pesticides and insecticides
■ secondary smoke
■ certain over-the-counter medications
■ electromagnetic fields, such as those created by heating pads and electric blankets
■ caffeine

Because many substances can, and do, cross the placental barrier, women who are even contemplating pregnancy should avoid unnecessary contact with known teratogens. As noted earlier, fetal organs and body systems are especially vulnerable

teratogens—harmful agents that can cause fetal damage (e.g., malformations, neurological, behavioral problems) during the prenatal period.

Table 3-2 Examples of Potentially Teratogenic Medications

- analgesics (more than an occasional dose of aspirin or ibuprofen)
- antibiotics (particularly tetracyclines and streptomycin)
- anticonvulsants (such as Dilantin)
- anticoagulants (used to thin the blood; such as Coumadin)
- antidepressants
- antihistamines
- antihypertensives (used to treat high blood pressure)
- antineoplastic drugs (used to treat cancers and some forms of arthritis; such as Methotrexate)
- antiviral agents
- hormones (such as diethylstilbesterol [DES] and progesterin)
- large doses of vitamin A (in excess of 10,000 IU); this includes some acne treatments, such as Accutane and Retin-A
- thyroid and antithyroid drugs

to such agents during the first weeks following conception. This is not to imply that there is ever a completely "safe" period. Even in the later months, fetal growth can be seriously affected by maternal exposure to, or use of, substances mentioned here and in the following sections.

Alcohol

Alcohol consumption during pregnancy can have serious consequences for both the mother and the developing fetus. Warnings to this effect now appear on the labels of all alcoholic products. Mothers who consume alcohol during pregnancy have a greater risk of miscarriages, stillbirths, premature babies, and low birth weight babies. The incidence of fetal death is also significantly higher. Because alcoholic beverages contain only calories and no nutrients, drinking them on a regular or binge basis may limit the mother's dietary intake of proteins, vitamins, and minerals necessary for her well-being, as well as that of her baby's.

Alcohol is also a potentially toxic teratogen that can have serious, irreversible effects on the fetus. Because mother and baby share a common circulatory system (via the placenta and umbilical cord), both are affected by any alcohol consumed. Alcohol is particularly damaging to the fetus during the critical first trimester of pregnancy, when many body structures and organs are being formed. It can result in preventable conditions known as fetal alcohol syndrome (FAS) and fetal alcohol effect (FAE, a milder form), causing mental and growth retardation, behavior and learning problems (hyperactivity), neurological limitations, heart defects, characteristic facial deformities, and speech impairments. When consumed later in the pregnancy, alcohol typically interferes with proper fetal growth.

How much alcohol may be damaging to an unborn child has not been determined. Most likely the relationship between alcohol and fetal damage is more complex than it may initially appear. Thus, no amount of alcohol is considered safe to consume during pregnancy.

Smoking

Fetal malformations and birth complications have also been linked to maternal smoking. Thus, warnings to this effect have been issued by the U.S. Surgeon General and are printed on all tobacco products. Cigarette smoke contains substances, such as nicotine, tars, and carbon monoxide, which cross the placental barrier and interfere with normal fetal development. Carbon monoxide, for example, reduces the amount of oxygen available to the fetus. This early oxygen deprivation seems to correlate with learning and behavior problems, especially as exposed children reach school age. Babies born to mothers who smoke are more likely to be of below-average weight, miscarried, premature, stillborn, and at higher risk for sudden infant death syndrome (SIDS), and also experience a higher rate of respiratory problems (e.g., allergies, asthma, colds).

Chemicals and Drugs

Numerous chemicals and drugs are also known to have an adverse effect on the developing fetus. These substances range from prescription and nonprescription medications to pesticides and "street" drugs. Some cause severe malformations, such as missing or malformed limbs or facial features. Others can lead to fetal death (spontaneous abortion), premature birth, or behavior and learning disabilities during childhood and youth. Not all exposed fetuses will be affected in the same manner or to the same degree. The nature and severity of an infant's abnormalities seem to be influenced by the timing of exposure during fetal development, as well as the amount and type of substance. Research has not yet provided a definitive answer as to which drugs and chemicals (if any) have absolutely no harmful effects on the developing fetus; therefore, women who are or may become pregnant should be extremely cautious about using any chemical substance or medication except under medical supervision. They should also avoid exposure to previously discussed environmental hazards, particularly in the early stages of pregnancy.

Maternal Infections

While the placenta effectively filters out many infectious organisms, it cannot prevent all disease-causing agents from reaching the unborn child. Some of these agents are known to cause fetal abnormalities; Table 3-3. Whether a fetus will be affected, and the type of abnormality, depends on the particular illness and stage of pregnancy when the infection occurs. For example, a pregnant woman who

Table 3-3 Examples of Potentially Teratogenic Maternal Conditions and Infections

- chickenpox
- cytomegalovirus (CMV)
- diabetes
- Fifth's disease
- herpes
- HIV
- mumps
- Rubella (German measles)
- syphilis
- toxoplasmosis

Note: Information about any of these infectious illnesses can be found on the Centers for Disease Control's Web site: www.cdc.gov/health/diseases.

develops rubella (German measles) during the first four to eight weeks following conception is at high risk for giving birth to an infant who has heart problems, or is deaf, blind, or both (an example of the extreme vulnerability of the fetus during its earliest weeks). *Note:* Rubella can be controlled if women who do not have natural immunity receive vaccinations after or not less than three to four months prior to pregnancy.

Fortunately, only a small percentage of babies exposed to infectious agents will experience abnormalities. It is still unknown why only some babies are affected, while others are not. What is reasonably certain is that pregnant women who are well nourished, have good prenatal care, and are generally healthy and free of addictive substances and other excesses have a high probability of giving birth to a strong and healthy baby.

SUMMARY

A human pregnancy requires approximately 266 days (nine months) from conception until a baby is fully developed. The mother's general health, age, quality of diet, emotional state, and physical fitness influence healthy fetal development. Exposure to environmental factors (teratogens), such as certain infectious illnesses, alcohol, addictive drugs, smoking, and some medications (prescription and over-the-counter) can have a harmful effect. Mothers can take steps to improve their chances of having a healthy pregnancy (and baby) by obtaining routine prenatal care, maintaining good health, following a nutritious diet, gaining an appropriate amount of weight (not too much or too little), participating in routine exercise, and maintaining a positive state of mental health.

KEY TERMS

amniocentesis   implantation

conception   placenta

CVS   sonogram

embryo   teratogens

genes

APPLY YOUR KNOWLEDGE

A. Apply What You Have Learned

Reread the developmental sketch about Anna and Miguel at the beginning of the chapter. How might you answer the following questions?

1. What stage of pregnancy is Anna currently experiencing?

2. What developmental features are characteristic of a fetus at three months?

3. At what point is Anna likely to begin feeling the baby move?

4. If you were Anna's doctor, what recommendations would you make for improving her chances of having a healthy baby?

5. What practices should Anna avoid during pregnancy to improve her chances of having a healthy baby?

6. What negative effects might Anna's smoking have on her pregnancy?

7. Which nutrients are especially important for Anna to include in her daily diet?

B. Review Questions

1. Identify three practices that promote a healthy pregnancy.

2. List three factors that appear to be hazardous to fetal development.

3. Identify one characteristic of fetal development that occurs during each stage.

4. What role(s) does the placenta play during pregnancy?

HELPFUL WEB SITES

American Dietetics Association	http://www.eatright.org
Centers for Disease Control and Prevention	http://www.cdc.gov/health/diseases.htm
Health Canada	http://www.hc-sc.gc.ca/hppb/nutrition
LeLeche League	http://www.lalecheleague.org
March of Dimes	http://www.modimes.org
National Agriculture Library	http://www.nal.usda.gov/fnic/Fpyr/pyramid
National Organization on Fetal Alcohol Syndrome	http://www.nofas.org
Women, Infants, and Children (WIC)	http://www.fns.usda.gov/wic

For additional child development resources, visit our Web site www.earlychilded.delmar.com

Infancy

 OBJECTIVES

After reading this chapter, you should be able to:

- Compare and contrast the physical characteristics of a typical four-month-old with those of a ten-month-old infant.
- Define the term *reflexive motor activity* and provide at least four examples.
- Explain why a four-week-old baby appears to walk when held in a standing position.
- React to the statement that "babies can't learn."
- Discuss ways in which babies communicate with adults.
- Identify five activities for promoting cognitive development with a four-week-old infant.
- Explain the phenomenon known as "stranger anxiety."

MEET JUAN

Anna and Miguel beamed as they watched their infant son, Juan, sleeping. Anna is thankful that her pregnancy went smoothly and that Juan is healthy despite being born almost two weeks early. Their family and friends often tell them what a "good baby" Juan seems to be. He sleeps three to four hours between feedings, follows their every movement, is discovering his fingers and toes, and often falls peacefully asleep in his father's arms.

Juan's parents can't believe their son will already turn two months old next week. When placed on his stomach, he tries to pick up his head to study the brightly colored geometric pictures his mother has fastened to the sides of the crib. He is also beginning to reach and grasp the small stuffed toys his parents offer to him. Anna is fascinated by how much Juan seems to be learning each day. Their pediatrician is also pleased with Juan's rate of growth and development.

Anna's maternity leave will soon end. She finds it difficult to think about returning to her job at the bank and having to leave Juan. However, she finds some comfort in the fact that Miguel's mother, having raised four children of her own, has offered to care for Juan until they are able to locate space in a nearby child care center. Juan's parents have visited several neighborhood programs and placed his name on waiting lists, but none have openings for an infant at this time.

The Newborn (Birth to One Month)

The healthy newborn infant is truly amazing. Within moments of birth it begins to adapt to an outside world that is radically different from the one experienced in **utero.** All body systems are in place and ready to function at birth. The newborn's body immediately assumes responsibility for breathing, eating, elimination, and regulation of body temperature. However, these systems are still quite immature, thus making the newborn completely dependent on parents and caregivers for survival.

Motor development (movement) is both reflexive and protective. There is no voluntary control of the body during the early weeks. Although newborn babies sleep most of the time, they do not lack awareness. They are sensitive to their environment and have unique methods of responding to it. Crying is their primary method for communicating needs and emotions. Perceptual and cognitive abilities are present, but they are primitive and relatively impossible to distinguish from one another.

Developmental Profiles and Growth Patterns

Growth and Physical Characteristics

The newborn's physical characteristics are unique from those of a slightly older infant. At birth the skin may appear wrinkled. Within the first few days it will dry out and possibly peel in some areas. Skin color of all babies is relatively light, but will gradually darken to a shade characteristic of their genetic background. The

---

in utero—the period when a fetus is developing in the mother's uterus.

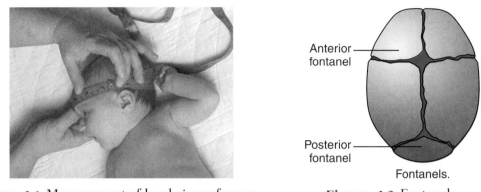

Figure 4-1 Measurement of head circumference.

Fontanels.

Figure 4-2 Fontanels.

head may appear to have an unusual shape as the result of the birth process, but it begins to assume a relatively normal shape within the first week. Hair color and amount vary.

- Weight at birth averages 6.5 to 9 pounds (3.0–4.1 kg); females weigh approximately 7 pounds (3.2 kg), males 7.5 pounds (3.4 kg).
- 5 to 7 percent of birth weight is lost in the days immediately following birth.
- Gains an average of 5 to 6 ounces (0.14–0.17 kg) per week during the first month.
- Length at birth ranges between 18 and 21 inches (45.7–53.3 cm).
- Respiration rate is approximately thirty to fifty breaths per minute; breathing may be somewhat irregular in rhythm and rate.
- Chest appears small and cylindrical; it is nearly the same size as the head.
- Normal body temperature ranges from 96°F to 99°F (35.6°C–37.2°C).
- Body temperature is irregular during the first few weeks due to immature body systems and a thin fat layer beneath the skin.
- Skin is sensitive, especially on the hands and mouth.
- Head is large in relation to body; accounts for nearly one-fourth of the total body length.
- Head circumference averages 12.5 to 14.5 inches (31.7–36.8 cm) at birth; Figure 4-1.
- "Soft" spots (**fontanels**) are located on the top (anterior) and back (posterior) of the head; Figure 4-2.
- Tongue appears large in proportion to mouth.
- Cries without tears.
- Eyes are extremely sensitive to light.
- Sees outlines and shapes; unable to focus on distant objects.

fontanels—small openings (sometimes called "soft spots") in the infant's skull bones, covered with soft tissue. Eventually they grow closed.

Motor Development

The newborn's motor skills are purely **reflexive** movements that are designed primarily for protection and survival. During the first month, the infant gains some control over several of these early reflexes. Gradually, many of these reflexes disappear as the infant's central nervous system matures and begins to take over control of purposeful behavior. During the first month the infant

■ Engages in motor activity that is primarily reflexive:
   —Swallowing, sucking, gagging, coughing, yawning, blinking, and elimination reflexes are present at birth.
   —Rooting reflex is triggered by gently touching the sensitive skin around the cheek and mouth; the infant turns toward the cheek being stroked.
   —Moro (startle) reflex is set off by a sudden loud noise or touch, such as bumping of the crib, or quick lowering of the infant's position downward (as if dropping); both arms are thrown open and away from the body, then quickly brought back together over the chest.
   —Grasping reflex occurs when the infant tightly curls its fingers around an object placed in its hand.
   —Stepping reflex involves the infant moving the feet up and down in walking-like movements when held upright with feet touching a firm surface; Figure 4-3.
   —Tonic neck reflex (TNR) occurs when the infant, in supine (face up) position, extends arm and leg on the same side toward which the head is turned; the opposite arm and leg are flexed (pulled in toward the body). This is sometimes called the "fencing position"; Figure 4-4.
   —Plantar reflex is initiated when pressure is placed against the ball of the infant's foot, causing the toes to curl.
■ Maintains "fetal" position (back flexed or rounded, extremities held close to the body, knees drawn up), especially when asleep.
■ Holds hands in a fist; does not reach for objects.
■ When held in a prone (face down) position, baby's head falls lower than the horizontal line of the body with hips flexed and arms and legs hanging down; Figure 4-5.
■ Has good muscle tone in the upper body when supported under the arms.
■ Turns head from side to side when placed in a prone position.
■ **Pupils** dilate (enlarge) and constrict (become smaller) in response to light.
■ Eyes do not always work together and may appear crossed at times.

---

reflexive—movements resulting from impulses of the nervous system that cannot be controlled by the individual.
pupil—the small, dark, central portion of the eye.

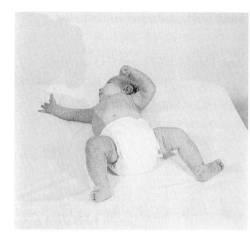

Figure 4-4 Tonic neck reflex (TNR).

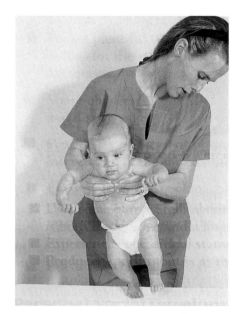

Figure 4-3 Stepping reflex.

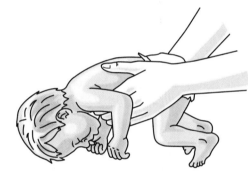

Figure 4-5 Prone suspension.

■ Attempts to track (follow) objects that are out of direct line of vision; unable to coordinate eye and hand movements.

Perceptual-Cognitive Development

The newborn's perceptual-cognitive skills are designed to capture and hold the attention of parents and caregivers and to gain some sense of the environment. Hearing is the most well developed of the skills. Newborns can hear and respond to differences among certain sounds and are especially responsive to their mother's voice. Sounds and movements, such as cooing, rocking, and jiggling, are often soothing. Newborns also are responsive to touch, with skin around the mouth and hands being especially sensitive. Vision is present, although limited. They are especially attracted to highly contrasting (black/white) geometric designs. The newborn

Figure 4-6 Begins to study own hand.

can focus both eyes, see objects up close, and follow slowly moving objects. From the earliest days of life, newborns absorb information through all of their senses, learning from what they see, hear, touch, taste, and smell. The newborn's cognitive behaviors can, thus, be characterized as purely reflexive. These take the form of sucking, startle responses, grimacing, flailing of arms and legs, and uncontrolled eye movements, all of which overlap with perceptual responses. During the first month the infant:

- Blinks eyes in response to fast-approaching object.
- Follows a slowly moving object through a complete 180-degree arc.
- Follows objects moved vertically if object is close to infant's face (10–15 inches [25.4–38.1 cm]).
- Continues looking about, even in the dark.
- Begins to study own hand when lying in TNR position; Figure 4-6.
- Hears as well (with the exception of quiet sounds) at birth as do most adults; hearing is more acute than vision.
- Prefers to listen to mother's voice rather than a stranger's.
- Often synchronizes body movements to speech patterns of parent or care-giver.
- Distinguishes some tastes; shows preference for sweet liquids.
- Has a keen sense of smell present at birth; will turn away from strong, unpleas-ant odors.

Speech and Language Development

The beginnings of speech and language development can be identified in several of the newborn's reflexes. These include the bite-release action that occurs when the infant's gums are rubbed, the rooting reflex, and the sucking reflex. In addition, the new baby communicates directly and indirectly in a number of other ways.

- Crying and fussing are major forms of communication at this stage.
- Reacts to loud noises by blinking, moving, stopping a movement, shifting eyes about, or making a startle response.

- Shows a preference for certain sounds, such as music and human voices, by calming down or quieting.
- Turns head in an effort to locate voices and other sounds.
- Makes occasional sounds other than crying.

Personal-Social Development

Newborns possess a variety of built-in social skills. They indicate needs and distress and respond to parents' or caregivers' reactions. The infant thrives on feelings of security, and soon displays a sense of attachment to primary caregivers. The newborn:

- Experiences a short period of alertness immediately following birth.
- Sleeps seventeen to nineteen hours a day; is gradually awake and responsive for longer periods.
- Likes to be held close and cuddled when awake.
- Shows qualities of individuality; each infant varies in ways of responding or not responding to similar situations.
- Begins to establish emotional attachment or a **bonding** relationship with parents and caregivers.
- Begins to develop a sense of security or trust with parents and caregivers; responses to different individuals vary. For example, an infant may become tense with an adult who is unfamiliar or uncomfortable with the infant.

Daily Routines

Birth to One Month

Eating

- Takes six to ten feedings, totaling approximately 22 ounces (660 ml) per twenty-four hours at the beginning of this period; later, the number of feedings will decrease to five or six as the amount consumed increases.
- Drinks 2 to 4 ounces of breast milk or formula per feeding; takes twenty-five to thirty minutes to complete a feeding; may fall asleep toward the end.
- Expresses the need for food by crying.
- Benefits from being fed in an upright position; this practice lessens the risk of choking and of developing ear infections.

bonding—the establishment of a close, loving relationship between an infant and adult, usually the mother and father; sometimes called attachment.

Toileting, Bathing, Dressing

- Signals the need for diaper change by crying (if crying does not stop when diaper has been changed, another cause should be sought).
- Enjoys bath; keeps eyes open and gives other indications of pleasure when placed in warm water.
- Expresses displeasure when clothes are pulled over head (best to avoid over-the-head clothes).
- Enjoys being wrapped firmly (swaddled) in a blanket; swaddling seems to foster feelings of security and comfort.
- Has one to four bowel movements per day.

Sleeping

- Begins to sleep four to six periods per twenty-four hours after the first few days following birth; one of these may be five to seven hours in length.
- Placing baby on back or side (propped) on firm mattress to sleep reduces the risk of sudden infant death syndrome (SIDS).
- Cries sometimes before falling asleep (usually stops if held and rocked briefly).

Play and Social Activities

- Enjoys light and brightness; may fuss if turned away from the light.
- Stares at faces in close visual range (10–12 inches [25.4–30.5 cm]).
- Signals the need for social stimulation by crying; stops when picked up or put in infant seat close to voices and movement.
- Is content to lie on back much of the time.
- Needs to be forewarned (e.g., touched, talked to) before being picked up.
- Enjoys lots of touching and holding; however, may become fussy with overstimulation.
- Enjoys "en face" (face-to-face) position.

Learning Activities

Tips for parents and teachers:

- Respond with gentle and dependable attention to baby's cries so baby learns that help is always available (infants always cry for a reason; crying signals a need).

- Make eye-to-eye contact when baby is in an alert state; make faces or stick out your tongue, activities that new babies often imitate (imitation is an important avenue for early learning).

- Talk or sing to a baby in a normal voice during feeding, diapering, and bathing; vary voice tone and rhythm of speech.

■ Recognize and show delight in baby's responsiveness. (Mutual responsive-ness and social turn-taking are the bases for all teaching and learning in the months and years ahead.)

■ Show baby simple pictures (new babies tend to prefer simple geometric designs and drawings of faces); gently move a stuffed animal or toy 10 to 15 inches (28–37.5 cm) from baby's face to encourage visual tracking; hang toys or mobile within baby's visual range (change often—novelty increases fascination).

■ Take cues from baby; too much stimulation can be as distressing as too little.

Developmenal Alerts

Check with a health care provider or early childhood specialist if, by one month of age, the infant *does not*:

■ Show alarm or "startle" responses to loud noise.

■ Suck and swallow with ease.

■ Show gains in height, weight, and head circumference.

■ Grasp with equal strength with both hands.

■ Make eye-to-eye contact when awake and being held.

■ Become quiet soon after being picked up.

■ Roll head from side to side when placed on stomach.

■ Express needs and emotions with cries and patterns of vocalizations that can be distinguished from one another.

■ Stop crying when picked up and held.

Safety Concerns

Before the baby arrives, complete first aid and cardiopulmonary resuscitation (CPR) courses. Be aware of new safety issues as the baby continues to grow and develop:

Burns

■ Never heat baby bottles in a microwave oven; hot spots can form and burn baby's mouth.

■ Set temperature of hot water heater no higher than 120°F.

■ Always check temperature of water before bathing baby.

Choking

■ Learn CPR.

■ Always hold infant while feeding; do not prop bottles.

Suffocation

■ Provide a firm mattress that fits crib snugly to prevent infant from becoming wedged in open cracks.

■ Always put baby to sleep on his or her back or side (propped); this practice reduces the risk of sudden infant death syndrome (SIDS). Tuck bottom edges of a light blanket under bottom end of mattress.

■ Remove soft items, such as fluffy blankets, stuffed animals, or pillows, from baby's crib.

■ Install smoke and carbon monoxide detectors near baby's room.

Transportation

■ Always use approved, rear-facing carrier when transporting baby in a vehicle; check for proper installation.

 # One to Four Months

During these early months, the wonders of infancy continue to unfold. Growth proceeds at a rapid pace. Body systems are fairly well stabilized, with temperature, breathing patterns, and heart rate becoming more regular. Motor skill improves as strength and voluntary muscle control increase. Longer periods of wakefulness encourage the infant's personal-social development. Social responsiveness begins to appear as infants practice and enjoy using their eyes to explore the environment. As social awareness develops, the infant gradually establishes a sense of trust and emotional attachment to parents and caregivers.

While crying remains a primary way of communicating and of gaining adult attention, more complex communication skills are gradually emerging. Infants begin to find great pleasure in imitating the speech sounds and gestures of others. Learning takes place continuously throughout the infant's waking hours as newly acquired skills are used for exploring and gathering information about a still new and unfamiliar environment. Providing baby with numerous opportunities for learning is important for fostering critical brain development (see Learning Activities). However, it is important to note once again that perceptual, cognitive, and motor development are closely interrelated and nearly impossible to differentiate during these early months.

Developmental Profiles and Growth Patterns

Growth and Physical Characteristics

■ Averages 20 to 27 inches (50.8–68.6 cm) in length; grows approximately one inch (2.54 cm) per month (measured with infant lying on back, from top of the head to bottom of heel, knees straight and foot flexed).

■ Weighs an average of 8 to 16 pounds (3.6–7.3 kg); females weigh slightly less than males.

■ Gains approximately 1/4 to 1/2 pound (0.11–0.22 kg) per week.

■ Breathes at a rate of approximately thirty to forty breaths per minute; rate increases significantly during periods of crying or activity.

■ Normal body temperature ranges from 96.4°F to 99.6°F (35.7°C–37.5°C).

■ Head and chest circumference are nearly equal.

■ Head circumference increases approximately 3/4 inch (1.9 cm) per month until two months, then increases 5/8 inch (1.6 cm) per month until four months. Increases are an important indication of continued brain growth.

■ Continues to breathe using abdominal muscles.

■ Posterior fontanel closes by the second month.

■ Anterior fontanel closes to approximately 1/2 inch (1.3 cm).

■ Skin remains sensitive and easily irritated.

■ Arms and legs are of equal length, size, and shape; easily flexed and extended.

■ Legs may appear slightly bowed.

■ Feet appear flat with no arch.

■ Cries with tears.

■ Begins moving eyes together in unison (binocular vision).

■ Color vision is present.

Motor Development

■ Reflexive motor behaviors are changing:
—Tonic neck and stepping reflexes disappear.
—Rooting and sucking reflexes are well developed.

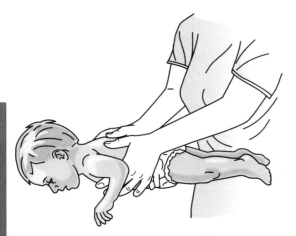

Figure 4-7 Landau reflex.

Figure 4-8 Begins to raise up on arms.

—Swallowing reflex and tongue movements are still immature; continued drooling and inability to move food to the back of the mouth.

—Grasp reflex gradually disappears.

—Landau reflex appears near the middle of this period; when baby is held in a prone (face down) position, the head is held upright and legs are fully extended; Figure 4-7.

■ Grasps with entire hand; strength insufficient to hold items.

■ Holds hands in an open or semi-open position.

■ Muscle tone and development are equal for boys and girls.

■ Movements tend to be large and jerky, gradually becoming smoother and more purposeful as muscle strength and control improve.

■ Raises head and upper body on arms when in a prone position; Figure 4-8.

■ Turns head side to side when in a supine (face up) position; near the end of this period can hold head up and in line with the body.

■ Shows greater activity level in upper body parts: clasps hands above face, waves arms about, reaches for objects.

■ Begins rolling from front to back by turning head to one side and allowing trunk to follow. Near the end of this period, infant can roll from front to back to side at will.

■ Can be pulled to a sitting position, with considerable head lag and rounded back at the beginning of this period; Figure 4-9. Later, can be positioned to sit, with minimal head support. By four months, most infants can sit with support, holding their head steady and keeping back fairly erect; enjoys sitting in an infant seat or being held on a lap.

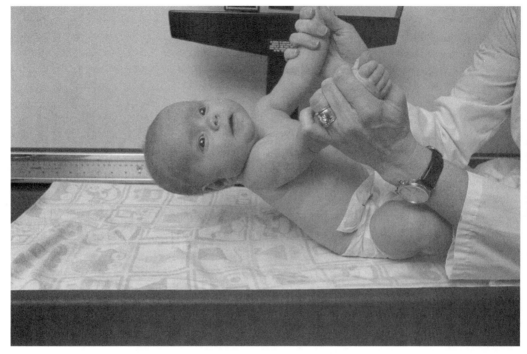

Figure 4-9 Can be pulled to a sitting position.

Perceptual-Cognitive Development

■ Fixates on a moving object held at a distance of 12 inches (30.5 cm); smoother visual tracking of objects across 180-degree pathway, vertically and horizontally.

■ Continues to gaze in direction of moving objects that have disappeared.

■ Exhibits some sense of size, color, and shape recognition of objects in the immediate environment—for example, recognizes own bottle even when bottle is turned about, thus presenting a different shape.

■ Does not search for a bottle that falls out of a crib or for a toy hidden under a blanket: "out of sight, out of mind." (The infant has not developed what Piaget refers to as **object permanence.**)

■ Watches hands intently.

■ Moves eyes from one object to another.

---

object permanence—*Piaget's sensorimotor stage when infants understand that an object exists even when it is not in sight.*

Figure 4-10 Focuses and reaches for objects.

■ Focuses on small object and reaches for it; usually follows own hand movements; Figure 4-10.

■ Alternates looking at an object, at one or both hands, and then back at the object.

■ Imitates gestures that are modeled: bye-bye, patting head.

■ Hits at object closest to right or left hand with some degree of accuracy.

■ Looks in the direction of a sound source (sound localization).

■ Connects sound and rhythms with movement by moving or jiggling in time to music, singing, or chanting.

■ Distinguishes parent's face from stranger's face when other cues, such as voice, touch, or smell, are also available.

■ Attempts to keep toy in motion by repeating arm or leg movements that started the toy moving in the first place.

■ Begins to mouth objects.

Speech and Language Development

■ Reacts (stops whimpering, startles) to sounds, such as a voice, rattle, or doorbell. Later, will search for source by turning head and looking in the direction of sound; Figure 4-11.

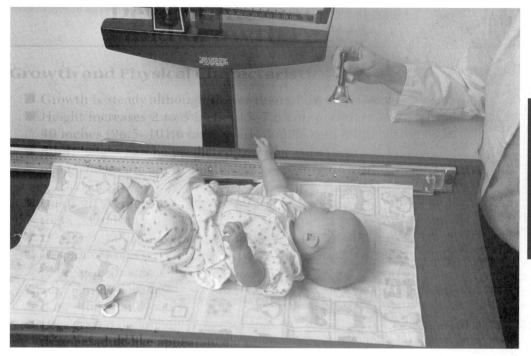

Figure 4-11 Turns toward sound.

■ Coordinates vocalizing, looking, and body movements in face-to-face exchanges with parent or caregiver; can follow and lead in keeping communication going.

■ Babbles or coos when spoken to or smiled at.

■ Coos using single vowel sounds (*ah, eh, uh*); also imitates own sounds and vowel sounds produced by others.

■ Laughs out loud.

Personal-Social Development

■ Imitates, maintains, terminates, and avoids interactions—for example, infants can turn at will toward or away from a person or situation.

■ Reacts differently to variations in adult voices; for example, may frown or look anxious if voices are loud, angry, or unfamiliar.

■ Enjoys being held and cuddled at times other than feeding and bedtime.

■ Coos, gurgles, and squeals when awake.

■ Smiles in response to a friendly face or voice; smiles occurring during sleep are thought to be reflexive.

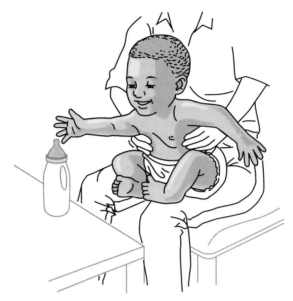

Figure 4-12 Recognizes and enjoys familiar routines.

■ Entertains self for brief periods by playing with fingers, hands, and toes.
■ Enjoys familiar routines, such as being bathed and having diaper changed.
■ Delights in play that involves gentle tickling, laughing, and jiggling.
■ Spends much less time crying.
■ Recognizes and reaches out to familiar faces and objects, such as father or bottle; reacts by waving arms and squealing with excitement; Figure 4-12.
■ Stops crying when parent or caregiver comes near.

Daily Routines

One to Four Months

Eating

■ Takes five to eight feedings, (5 to 6 ounces each) per day.
■ Begins fussing before anticipated feeding times; does not always cry to signal the need to eat.

- Needs only a little assistance in getting nipple to mouth; beginning to help by using own hands to guide nipple.
- Sucks vigorously; may choke on occasion because of the vigor and enthusiasm of sucking.
- Becomes impatient if bottle or breast continues to be offered once hunger is satisfied.
- Requires only breast milk or formula to meet all nutrient needs; not ready to eat solid foods.

Toileting, Bathing, Dressing

- Enjoys bathtime on most occasions; kicks, laughs, and splashes.
- Has one or two bowel movements per day; may skip a day.
- Begins to establish a regular time or pattern for bowel movements.

Sleeping

- Falls asleep for the night soon after the evening feeding.
- Begins to sleep through the night; many babies do not sleep more than six hours at a stretch for several more months.
- Averages fourteen to seventeen hours of sleep per day; often awake for two or three periods during the daytime.
- Sometimes begins thumbsucking during this period.
- Begins to entertain self before falling asleep: "talks," plays with hands, jiggles crib.

Play and Social Activity

- Spends waking periods in physical activity: kicking, turning head from side to side, clasping hands together, grasping objects.
- Vocalizes with delight; becoming more "talkative."
- Likes being talked and sung to; may cry when the social interaction ends.
- Appears happy when awake and alone (for short periods of time).

Learning Activities

Tips for parents and teachers:

- Imitate baby's vocalizations and faces (grunting, smacking, yawning, squinting, frowning). When baby begins to smile, smile back and sometimes remark, "You are smiling! Great smile!"

■ Sing songs and read to baby out of magazines, books, whatever interests you; it's the sound of your voice and your closeness that matter.

■ Play simplified peek-a-boo (hold cloth in front of your own face, drop it, say *peek-a-boo*); repeat if baby shows interest.

■ Gently stretch and bend baby's arms and legs while making up an accompanying song; later, start a gentle "bicycling" activity.

■ Touch baby's hand with a small toy* (soft rattles or other noisemakers are especially good); encourage baby to grasp toy.

■ Walk around with baby, touching and naming objects. Stand with baby in front of mirror, touching and naming facial features: "Baby's mouth, Daddy's mouth. Baby's eye, Mommy's eye."

■ Attach an unbreakable mirror to crib or wall close to the crib so baby can look and talk to himself or herself.

■ Hang brightly colored or geometric pictures (black and white) or objects near baby's crib; change often to maintain baby's interest and attention.

■ Fasten (*securely*) small bells to baby's booties; this helps baby to localize sounds and learn, at the same time, that he or she has power and can make things happen simply by moving about.

***Rule of fist:* Toys and other objects given to an infant should be no smaller than the baby's fist (1.5 inches; 3.8 cm) to prevent choking or swallowing.**

Developmental Alerts

Check with a health care provider or early childhood specialist if, by four months of age, the infant *does not*:

■ Continue to show steady increases in height, weight, and head circumference.

■ Smile in response to the smiles of others (the social smile is a significant developmental milestone).

■ Follow a moving object with eyes focusing together.

■ Bring hands together over midchest.

■ Turn head to locate sounds.

- Begin to raise head and upper body when placed on stomach.
- Reach for objects or familiar persons.

Safety Concerns

Continue to implement Safety Concerns described for the previous stages. Be aware of new safety issues as the baby continues to grow and develop:

Burns

- Do not bring hot beverages or appliances near baby.

Choking

- Check rattles and stuffed toys for small parts that could become loose. Only purchase toys larger than l.5 inches (3.75 cm) in diameter.
- Remove all small items within baby's reach.

Falls

- Attend to baby at all times when on an elevated surface (e.g., changing table, sofa, counter, bed); baby may turn over or roll unexpectedly.
- Always place infant carriers on the floor (not on table or counter top).

Sharp Objects

- Keep pins and other sharp objects out of baby's reach.
- Check nursery furniture for sharp or protruding edges; always purchase furnishings and toys that comply with federal safety standards (see Helpful Web Sites).

Four to Eight Months

Between four and eight months, infants are developing a wide range of skills and greater ability to use their bodies. Infants seem to be busy every waking moment, manipulating and mouthing toys and other objects. They "talk" all the time, making vowel and consonant sounds in ever greater variety and complexity. They initi-

4 to 8 Months

ate social interactions and respond to all kinds of cues, such as facial expressions, gestures, and the comings and goings of everyone in their world. Infants at this age are both self-contained and sociable. They move easily from spontaneous, self-initiated activity to social activities initiated by others.

Developmental Profiles and Growth Patterns

Growth and Physical Characteristics

- Gains approximately one pound (2.2 kg) per month in weight.
- Doubles original birth weight.
- Increases length by approximately 1/2 inch (1.3 cm) per month; average length is 27.5 to 29 inches (69.8–73.7 cm).
- Head and chest circumferences are nearly equal.
- Increases in head circumference average 3/8 inch (0.95 cm) per month until six to seven months of age; this rate slows to approximately 3/16 inch (0.47 cm) per month. Head circumference should continue to increase steadily, indicating healthy, ongoing brain growth.
- Takes approximately twenty-five to fifty breaths per minute, depending on activity; rate and patterns vary from infant to infant; breathing is abdominal.
- Begins to cut teeth, with upper and lower incisors coming in first.
- Gums may become red and swollen, accompanied by increased drooling, chewing, biting, and mouthing of objects; Figure 4-13.
- Legs may appear bowed; bowing gradually disappears as infant grows older.
- Establishes true eye color.

Motor Development

- Reflexive behaviors are changing:
  —Blinking reflex is well established.
  —Sucking reflex becomes voluntary.
  —Moro reflex disappears.
  —Parachute reflex appears toward the end of this stage (when held in a prone, horizontal position and lowered suddenly, infant throws out arms as a protective measure); Figure 4-14.
  —Swallowing reflex appears (a more complex form of swallowing that involves tongue movement against the roof of mouth); allows infant to move solid foods from front of mouth to the back for swallowing.
- Uses finger and thumb (pincer grip) to pick up objects; Figure 4-15.

Figure 4-13 Chews and mouths objects.

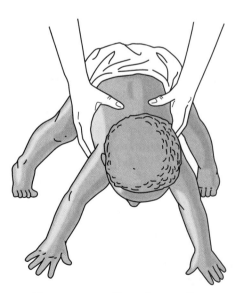

Figure 4-14 Parachute reflex.

Figure 4-15 Pincer grip.

- Reaches for objects with both arms simultaneously; later reaches with one hand or the other.
- Transfers objects from one hand to the other; grasps object using entire hand (palmar grasp).
- Handles, shakes, and pounds objects; puts everything in mouth.
- Holds own bottle.
- Sits alone without support, holding head erect, back straightened, and arms propped forward for support.
- Pulls self into a crawling position by raising up on arms and drawing knees up beneath the body; rocks back and forth, but generally does not move forward.
- Lifts head when placed on back.
- Rolls over from front to back and back to front.
- Begins scooting backward, sometimes accidentally, when placed on stomach; soon will learn to crawl forward.
- Enjoys being placed in standing position, especially on someone's lap; jumps in place.

Perceptual-Cognitive Development

- Turns toward and locates familiar voices and sounds: this behavior can be used to test an infant's hearing informally.
- Focuses eyes on small objects and reaches for them.
- Uses hand, mouth, and eyes in coordination to explore own body, toys, and surroundings.
- Imitates actions, such as pat-a-cake, waving bye-bye, and playing peek-a-boo.
- Shows fear of falling off high places, such as changing table, stairs; **depth perception** is clearly evident.
- Looks over side of crib or high chair for objects dropped; delights in repeatedly throwing objects overboard for adult to retrieve; Figure 4-16.
- Searches for toy or food that has been completely hidden under cloth or behind screen; beginning to understand that objects continue to exist even when they cannot be seen. (Piaget refers to this as object permanence.)
- Handles and explores objects in a variety of ways: visually; turning them around; feeling all surfaces; banging and shaking.
- Picks up inverted object (in other words, recognizes a cup even when it is positioned differently).
- Ignores second toy or drops toy in one hand when presented with a new toy; unable to deal with more than one toy at a time.
- Reaches accurately with either hand.

---

depth perception—ability to determine the relative distance of objects from the observer.

Figure 4-16 Enjoys throwing objects for adults to retrieve.

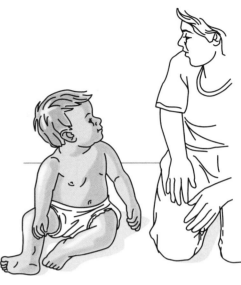

Figure 4-17 Recognizes and responds to own name.

4 to 8 Months

- Plays actively with small toys, such as rattle or block.
- Bangs objects together playfully; bangs spoon or toy on table.
- Continues to put everything in mouth.
- Establishes full attachment to mother or single caregiver which coincides with growing understanding of object permanence.

Speech and Language Development

- Responds appropriately to own name and simple requests, such as "eat," "wave bye-bye"; Figure 4-17.
- Imitates some nonspeech sounds, such as cough, tongue click, lip smacking.
- Produces a full range of vowels and some consonants: *r*, *s*, *z*, *th*, and *w*.
- Responds to variations in the tone of voice of others—anger, playfulness, sadness.
- Expresses emotions, such as pleasure, satisfaction, and anger, by making different sounds.
- "Talks" to toys.
- Babbles by repeating same syllable in a series: *ba, ba, ba.*
- Reacts differently to noises, such as a vacuum cleaner, phone ringing, or dog barking; may cry, whimper, or look for reassurance from parent or caregiver.

Figure 4-18 Still friendly with strangers.

Personal-Social Development

■ Delights in observing surroundings; continuously watches people and activities.

■ Begins to develop an awareness of self as a separate individual from others.

■ Becomes more outgoing and social in nature: smiles, coos, reaches out.

■ Distinguishes among, and responds differently, to strangers, teachers, parents, and siblings.

■ Responds differently and appropriately to facial expressions: frowns; smiles.

■ Imitates facial expressions, actions, and sounds.

■ Remains friendly toward strangers at the beginning of this stage; later, is reluctant to be approached by, or left with, strangers; exhibits "**stranger anxiety**"; Figure 4-18.

■ Enjoys being held and cuddled; indicates desire to be picked up by raising arms.

■ Establishes a trust relationship with parents and caregivers if physical and emotional needs are met consistently; by six months, begins to show preference for primary caregiver.

■ Laughs out loud.

■ Becomes upset if toy or other objects are taken away.

■ Seeks attention by using body movements, verbalizations, or both.

stranger anxiety—distress or fear shown when approached by unfamiliar persons.

Four to Eight Months

Eating

- Adjusts feeding times to the family's schedule; usually takes three or four feedings per day, each 6 to 8 ounces, depending on sleep schedule.
  Caution: Do not allow infants to drink formula or juice from a bottle for extended periods of time. Baby bottle tooth decay (BBTD) can result from prolonged contact with these fluids and cause extensive damage.
- Shows interest in feeding activities; reaches for cup and spoon while being fed.
- Able to wait half hour or more after awakening for first morning feeding.
- Has less need for sucking.
- Begins to accept small amount of pureed foods, such as cereal and vegetables, when placed well back on tongue (if placed on tip, infant will push food back out).
- Closes mouth firmly or turns head away when hunger is satisfied.

Toileting, Bathing, Dressing

- Enjoys being free of clothes.
- Splashes vigorously with both hands and sometimes feet during bathtime.
- Moves hands constantly; nothing within reach is safe from being spilled, placed in the mouth, or dashed to the floor.
- Pulls off own socks; plays with strings, buttons, and velcro closures on clothing.
- Has one bowel movement per day as a general rule, often at about the same time.
- Urinates often and in quantity; female infants tend to have longer intervals between wetting.

Sleeping

- Awakens between 6 and 8 A.M.; usually falls asleep soon after evening meal.
- Begins to give up need for a late-night feeding.
- Sleeps eleven to thirteen hours through the night.
- Takes two or three naps per day (however, there is great variability among infants in terms of frequency and length of naps).

Play and Social Activity

- Enjoys lying on back; arches back, kicks, stretches legs upward, grasps feet and brings them to mouth.
- Looks at own hands with interest and delight; may squeal or gaze at them intently.
- Enjoys playing with soft, squeaky toys and rattles; puts them in mouth, bites, and chews on them.
- "Talks" happily to self: gurgles, growls, makes high squealing sounds.
- Differentiates between people: lively with those who are familiar, anxious about, or ignores, others.
- Likes rhythmic activities: being bounced, jiggled, swayed about gently.

Learning Activities

Tips for parents and teachers:

■ Gradually elaborate on earlier activities: imitate baby's sounds, facial expressions, and body movements; name body parts; look in the mirror together and make faces; read, talk, and sing to baby throughout the day.

■ Use baby's name during all kinds of activities so baby comes to recognize it: "*Kyle* is smiling," "*Carla's* eyes are wide open."

■ Provide toys, rattles, and household items that make noise as baby shakes or waves them (a set of measuring spoons or plastic keys, shaker cans, squeak toys; remember the *"Rule of fist,"* p. 66.)

■ Fasten a cradle gym across the crib; a younger baby can swipe at objects and later actually connect (both activities are essential in learning eye–hand coordination). Homemade cradle gyms made of safe household items are equally effective.

■ Play and move to radio or taped music with baby; vary the tempo and movement: gentle jiggling, dancing, turning in circles; dance in front of the mirror, describing movements to baby.

■ Sing all types of songs to baby—silly songs, lullabies, popular tunes.

■ Allow plenty of time for bathtime. This activity provides an important opportunity for learning in all developmental areas, as well as an overall enjoyment of learning.

■ Play *This little piggy, Where's baby's* (nose, eye, hand . . .), and other simple games invented on the spot, such as taking turns at shaking rattles, gently rubbing foreheads, or clapping hands.

Developmental Alerts

Check with a health care provider or early childhood specialist if, by eight months of age, the infant *does not*:

■ Show even, steady increase in weight, height, and head size (too slow or too rapid growth are both causes for concern).

■ Explore own hands and objects placed in hands.

■ Hold and shake a rattle.

■ Smile, babble, and laugh out loud.

■ Search for hidden objects.

■ Use pincer grasp to pick up objects.

■ Have an interest in playing games, such as "pat-a-cake" and "peek-a-boo."

■ Appear interested in new or unusual sounds.

■ Reach for and grasp objects.

■ Sit alone.

■ Begin to eat some solid (pureed) foods.

Safety Concerns

Continue to implement Safety Concerns described for the previous stages. Be aware of new safety issues as the baby continues to grow and develop:

Burns

■ Keep electrical cords out of reach and electrical outlets covered; inspect the condition of electrical cords and replace or remove them if worn or frayed.

■ Take precautions to protect baby from accidentally touching hot objects, such as oven or fireplace doors, burning cigarettes, or hot beverage cups.

Falls

■ Use gates to protect baby from tumbling down stairs; gates are also useful for keeping baby confined to an area for supervision.

■ When using a highchair, always fasten the restraining straps.

■ Always raise crib sides to their maximum height and lock when baby is in bed.

Poisons

■ Use safety latches on cabinet doors and drawers where potentially poisonous substances (e.g., medications, cleaning supplies, cosmetics, garden chemicals) may be stored.

8 to 12 Months

Strangulation

■ Never fasten teethers or pacifiers on a cord or around baby's neck.

■ Remove crib gyms and mobiles after baby reaches five months or begins pushing up on hands and knees.

Eight to Twelve Months

Between eight and twelve months of age, the infant is gearing up for two major developmental events—walking and talking. These milestones usually begin about the time of the first birthday. The infant is increasingly able to manipulate small objects, and spends a great deal of time practicing by picking up and releasing toys or whatever else is at hand. Infants at this age are also becoming extremely sociable. They find ways to be the center of attention and to win approval and applause from family and friends. When applause is forthcoming, the infant joins in with delight. The ability to imitate improves and serves two purposes: to extend social interactions and to help the child learn many new skills and behaviors in the months of rapid development that lie ahead.

Developmental Profiles and Growth Patterns

Growth and Physical Characteristics

■ Gains in height are slower than during the previous months, averaging 1/2 inch (1.3 cm) per month. Infants reach approximately 1-1/2 times their birth length by the first birthday.

■ Weight increases by approximately one pound (0.5 kg) per month; birth weight nearly triples by one year of age: infants weigh an average of 21 pounds (9.6 kg).

■ Respiration rates vary with activity: typically, twenty to forty-five breaths per minute.

■ Body temperature ranges from 96.4°F to 99.6°F (35.7°C–37.5°C); environmental conditions, weather, activity, and clothing still affect variations in temperature.

■ Circumferences of head and chest remain equal.

■ Uses abdominal muscles for breathing.

■ Anterior fontanel begins to close.

■ Approximately four upper and four lower incisors and two lower molars erupt.

■ Arms and hands are more developed than feet and legs (cephalocaudal development); hands appear large in proportion to other body parts.

Diversity

The composition and character of American society is changing at a pace greater than at anytime in the past. Children attending early childhood programs mirror these societal changes and their growing diversity is representative of currents in the general population. For this reason, it is important to understand the multifaceted quality of diversity and its implications for developmentally appropriate practices.

THE NATURE OF DIVERSITY

Children are each unique in their own way; no two are ever precisely alike. The ongoing and complex interactions that occur between a child's genetic makeup, environments, and accumulation of life experiences are responsible for the differences that distinguish one child from another. It is this 'one-of-a-kindness,' or diversity, that accounts for the individuality of every child and adult.

In the broadest sense, the term diversity is inclusive, referring to a wide range of similarities, as well as differences. Dimensions that are most commonly described include:

- age
- gender
- race and ethnic background
- socio-economic class
- language
- abilities

However, diversity issues extend well beyond simple categorization.

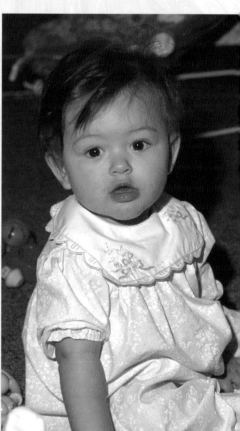

Family systems, communication styles, religious preferences, education, parenting practices, and community values all play important roles in shaping a child's unique heritage. They also influence a child's sense of identity, or self-concept. Each life experience affects the view children have of themselves. Therefore, efforts must be made to avoid simplistic assumptions and generalizations about aspects of diversity because there are often many variations associated with each dimension. For example, a child who speaks Spanish may come from any number of geographical locations or cultures. Categorizing a child as "Latino" fails to acknowledge individual and cultural differences and, thus, promotes stereotyping.

IMPLICATIONS FOR EARLY CHILDHOOD TEACHERS

Teachers clearly occupy key positions of influence with respect to diversity issues. Every phase of planning and implementation within early childhood programs becomes an opportunity for promoting a sense of understanding and acceptance of differences by children and adults. Teachers can help children begin to build a foundation that consists of positive attitudes and respect through classroom environments they create, their choices of activities and learning materials, and modeling of sensitive behavior.

VALUES AND ATTITUDES

It is always important for teachers to examine their own attitudes and beliefs about various cultures, practices, religions, abilities, and limitations in order to recognize potential biases. Personal ignorance and prejudice limit a teacher's effectiveness in promoting acceptance and celebration of individual differences in the classroom. This self-examination process also opens doors to opportunities for acquiring new information and improved understanding.

Early childhood settings present many valuable opportunities for helping children gain positive attitudes toward others. A value-neutral classroom environment encourages children to express their questions and curiosities about individual differences.

Answers given in a direct and objective manner promote an atmosphere of acceptance and respect. Activities that are integrated into daily learning experiences, rather than taught as separate and occasional lessons, help children develop a greater appreciation for diversity. Over time, children will learn to treat one another with respect, fairness, and friendship and to value the unique contributions of each individual.

COMMUNICATION

Quality early childhood programs are based on effective communication in a context that supports an appreciation of diversity. Teachers should encourage all children to communicate in whatever form their abilities allow. Teachers acknowledge and show respect for cultural variations in children's language, and provide learning experiences that value these differences.

Misunderstandings can be prevented when time is taken to learn the significance and variations of communication styles, including nonverbal behaviors such as facial expressions, eye contact, touch, and posture. Knowing, for example, that direct eye contact is considered disrespectful among some cultures and, therefore, is purposefully avoided, reduces the chance of misinterpreting this behavior as inattention, indifference, or rudeness.

Children's communication needs can be met through daily classroom experiences that embrace the richness of cultural differences. Activities, especially those involving art, music, storytelling, and dramatic play, facilitate children's mastery of basic communication skills. They are also effective for improving language proficiency, learning to ask questions, exploring differences, expressing opinions freely and, thus, broadening a child's social competency.

LEARNING EXPERIENCES

Educational programs that value diversity provide experiences that broaden children's understanding of other cultures and abilities. They also accommodate children's differences in interests and learning styles. Teachers recognize that children's personalities, skills, talents, language, and cultural backgrounds all influence the context in which they learn. Teachers know their children and select educational practices and instructional materials that are meaningful and relevant to the diverse nature of children. Teachers view families as valuable resources and encourage them to participate in their children's learning experiences. Every effort is made to avoid materials and practices that are disrespectful or support biased information.

ASSESSMENT

Evaluation of children's abilities and developmental progress also respects their diversity. Teachers choose assessment tools and practices that take into account differences in children's backgrounds, cultural expectations, learning styles, and physical, mental, and language limitations. They identify evaluation measures that acknowledge children's strengths, as well as their weaknesses. Observations of children in their natural settings are included so as to be sensitive to matters of diversity and to avoid tendencies for biased assumptions. Evaluation also includes the family, and takes their expectations into consideration when establishing realistic goals and objectives for children. Teachers who value diversity also recognize when circumstances make assessment inappropriate or invalid.

WORKING WITH FAMILIES

Programs that value diversity involve families in children's learning experiences. Family members are invited to share their traditions, language, celebrations, foods, music, stories, and special talents. They are welcomed at every opportunity — their presence and participation is encouraged and valued. Communication between families and teachers is frequent, supportive, respectful, and builds important partnerships.

Family involvement brings an unparalleled richness to early childhood programs, and enhances children's understanding and acceptance of individual differences. It also helps children develop a stronger sense of self-identity and self-worth. Similarly, families benefit from involvement in their children's education. Improved understanding and consistency result when ties are strengthened between children's homes and school.

The challenge clearly remains — to continue working toward greater understanding, sensitivity, and acceptance of individual differences.

Figure 4-19 Begins to pull up to a standing position.

- Legs may continue to appear bowed.
- Feet appear flat as arch has not yet fully developed.
- Visual acuity is approximately 20/100.
- Both eyes work in unison (true binocular coordination).
- Can see distant objects (15 to 20 feet away) and points at them.

Motor Development

- Reaches with one hand leading to grasp an offered object or toy.
- Manipulates objects, transferring them from one hand to the other.
- Explores new objects by poking with one finger.
- Uses deliberate pincer grip to pick up small objects, toys, and finger foods.
- Stacks objects; also places objects inside one another.
- Releases objects or toys by dropping or throwing; cannot intentionally put an object down.
- Begins pulling self to a standing position; Figure 4-19.
- Begins to stand alone, leaning on furniture for support; moves or "cruises" around obstacles by side-stepping.
- Maintains good balance when sitting; can shift positions without falling.
- Creeps on hands and knees; crawls up and down stairs.
- Walks with adult support, holding onto adult's hand; may begin to walk alone.

8 to 12 Months

Figure 4-20 Continues to put everything in the mouth.

Perceptual-Cognitive Development

- Watches people, objects, and activities in the immediate environment.
- Shows awareness of distant objects (15 to 20 feet away) by pointing at them.
- Responds to hearing tests (voice localization); however, loses interest quickly and, therefore, may be difficult to test informally.
- Follows simple instructions, such as "wave bye-bye," "clap hands."
- Reaches for toys that are visible but out of reach.
- Puts everything in mouth; Figure 4-20.
- Continues to drop first item when other toys or items are offered.
- Recognizes the reversal of an object: cup upside down is still a cup.
- Imitates activities: hitting two blocks together, playing pat-a-cake.
- Drops toys intentionally and repeatedly; looks in direction of fallen object.
- Shows appropriate use of everyday items: pretends to drink from cup, put on a necklace, hug doll, make stuffed animal "walk"; Figure 4-21.
- Shows some sense of spatial relationships: puts block in cup and takes it out when requested to do so.

Figure 4-21 Understands the use of everyday objects.

■ Begins to show an understanding of causality—for example, hands mechanical toy back to adult to have it rewound.
■ Shows some awareness of the functional relationship of objects; puts spoon in mouth, uses brush to smooth hair, turns pages of a book.
■ Searches for partially hidden toy by the end of this period.

Speech and Language Development

■ Babbles or jabbers deliberately to initiate social interaction; may shout to attract attention, listen, then shout again.
■ Shakes head for "no" and may nod for "yes."
■ Responds by looking for voice when name is called.
■ Babbles in sentence-like sequences; followed later by jargon (syllables and sounds with language-like inflection).
■ Waves "bye-bye"; claps hands when asked.
■ Says "da-da" and "ma-ma."
■ Imitates sounds that are similar to those the baby has already learned to make; will also imitate motor noises, tongue click, lip smacking, coughing.
■ Enjoys rhymes and simple songs; vocalizes and dances to music.
■ Hands toy or object to an adult when appropriate gestures accompany the request.

Personal-Social Development

■ Exhibits a definite fear of strangers; clings to, or hides behind, parent or caregiver ("stranger anxiety"); often resists separating from familiar adult ("separation anxiety").

■ Wants parent or caregiver to be in constant sight.

■ Enjoys being near, and included in, daily activities of family members and teachers; is becoming more sociable and outgoing.

■ Enjoys novel experiences and opportunities to examine new objects.

■ Shows need to be picked up and held by extending arms upward, crying, or clinging to adult's legs.

■ Begins to exhibit assertiveness by resisting caregiver's requests; may kick, scream, or throw self on the floor.

■ Offers toys and objects to others.

■ Often becomes attached to a favorite toy or blanket.

■ Looks up and smiles at person who is speaking upon hearing own name.

■ Repeats behaviors that get attention; jabbers continuously.

■ Carries out simple directions and requests; understands the meaning of "no."

Daily Routines

Eight to Twelve Months

8 to 12 Months

Eating

■ Eats three meals a day plus midmorning or midafternoon snacks, such as juice, fruit, crackers, and cereal.

■ Begins to refuse bottle (if this has not already occurred).

■ Enjoys eating and has a good appetite.

■ Likes to drink from a cup, holding it alone; will even tilt head backward to get the last drop.

■ Begins to eat finger foods; may remove food from mouth, look at it, put it back in.

■ Develops certain likes and dislikes for foods.

■ Continuously active; infant's hands may be so busy that a toy is needed for each hand in order to prevent cup or dish from being turned over or food grabbed and tossed.

Toileting, Bathing, Dressing

■ Enjoys bathtime; plays with washcloth, soap, and water toys.
■ Loves to let water drip from sponge or washcloth, pour water from cup to cup.
■ Shows great interest in pulling off hats, taking off shoes and socks.
■ Fusses when diaper needs changing; may pull off soiled or wet diaper.
■ Cooperates to some degree in being dressed; helps put arms in armholes, may even extend legs to have pants put on.
■ Has one or two bowel movements per day.
■ Remains dry after nap on occasion.

Sleeping

■ Goes to bed willingly; may not fall asleep immediately, but will play or walk about in crib, then fall asleep on top of covers.
■ Sleeps until 6 or 8 A.M.
■ Plays alone and quietly for fifteen to thirty minutes after awakening; then begins to make demanding noises, signaling the need to be up and about.
■ Plays actively in crib when awake; crib sides must be up and securely fastened.
■ Takes one afternoon nap most days; length varies from infant to infant.

Play and Social Activities

■ Enjoys large motor activities: pulling to stand, cruising, standing alone, creeping. Some babies are walking at this point.
■ Enjoys putting things on head: basket, bowl, cup; finds this very funny and expects people to notice and laugh.
■ Puts objects in and out of each other: pans that nest, toys in and out of a box.
■ Enjoys hiding behind chairs to play "Where's baby?"
■ Throws things on floor and expects them to be returned.
■ Shows interest in opening and closing doors and cupboards.
■ Gives an object to adult on request; expects to have it returned immediately.
■ Responds to "no-no" by stopping; on the other hand, the infant may smile, laugh, and continue inappropriate behavior, thus making a game out of it.

Learning Activities

Tips for parents and teachers:

■ Elaborate on activities suggested earlier; always pick up on baby's lead whenever baby initiates a new response or invents a new version of a familiar game (the roots of creativity).

8 to 12 Months

- Provide safe floor space close to parent or caregiver; learning to sit, crawl, stand, and explore are a baby's major tasks during these months.

- Read and tell short stories about everyday happenings in baby's life; also read from sturdy, brightly colored picture books, allowing baby to help turn the pages.

- Talk about ongoing activities, emphasizing key words: "Here is the *soap*," "You are *squeezing* the sponge," "Let's wash hands before you eat."

- Give baby simple instructions: "Pat Mommy's head," "Pat baby's head." Allow adequate time for response; if baby seems interested, but does not respond, demonstrate the response.

- Accept baby's newly invented game of dropping things off highchair or tray or out of the crib; it's baby's way of learning about many things: cause and effect, gravity, adults' patience.

- Provide containers that baby can fill with small toys or other objects and then empty out. ("Rule of fist" still applies.)

- Give baby push and pull toys, roly-polies, toys with wheels. (Helping to unpack canned goods and rolling them across the kitchen floor is an all-time favorite game.)

Developmental Alerts

Check with a health care provider or early childhood specialist if, by twelve months of age, the infant *does not*:

- Blink when fast-moving objects approach the eyes.

- Begin to cut teeth.

- Imitate simple sounds.

- Follow simple verbal requests: *come, bye-bye.*

- Pull self to a standing position.

- Transfer objects from hand to hand.

- Show anxiety toward strangers.

- Interact playfully with parents, caregivers, and siblings.

- Feed self; hold own bottle or cup; pick up and eat finger foods.

- Creep or crawl on hands and knees.

Safety Conerns

Continue to implement Safety Concerns described for the previous stages. Be aware of new safety issues as the baby continues to grow and develop:

Choking

■ Cut finger foods into small bites (1/4 inch [0.63 cm] or smaller).

■ Keep small objects, such as buttons, dry cat food, coins, and pen tops out of baby's reach; keep garbage cans closed tightly. *Any item that fits through a toilet paper tube is too small for young children.*

Drowning

■ Remove unsupervised sources of water, including fountains, pet dishes, and wading pools; place safety devices on toilet lids.

Falls

■ Never allow baby to stand up in a highchair, grocery shopping cart, or on the changing table (unless you are holding onto baby).

■ Pad sharp corners and edges of furniture and cabinet doors.

Strangulation

■ Purchase clothing, such as jackets, with elastic instead of pull strings in the hoods.

■ Fasten cords on all blinds and curtains up high and out of children's reach.

Suffocation

■ Keep plastic bags and wrappings out of baby's reach; knot them and discard immediately.

SUMMARY

The span between birth and a child's first birthday is marked by dramatic changes in all developmental areas. Gains in height and weight occur at a rate greater than at any other time during the lifespan. Good nutrition plays a key role in assuring healthy growth; malnutrition may severely limit this growth potential. Evolving changes in physical development, coupled with rapidly improving motor skills, transform the infant from a nonambulatory, reflexive state to one over which the child begins to master some purposeful control. This period also marks one of the most important stages of brain development in terms of size (actual number of

8 to 12 Months

brain cells) and the establishment of nerve connections—both of which are essential for the acquisition of speech and language as well as perceptual-cognitive, motor, and personal-social abilities. Many factors influence this learning process, including genetics, culture, environment, and the expectations of individuals with whom the infant interacts.

 KEY TERMS

bonding	object permanence
depth perception	pupil
fontanels	reflexive
in utero	stranger anxiety

APPLY YOUR KNOWLEDGE

A. Apply What You Have Learned

Reread the developmental sketch about Juan and his parents, Anna and Miguel, at the beginning of the chapter. How might you answer the following questions?

1. Based on what you have learned in this chapter, would you consider Juan's development to be progressing typically for his age? Explain.

2. Should you expect Juan to still be waking up for nighttime feedings at this age?

3. What activities can Anna and Miguel begin doing now to encourage Juan's long-term language development?

4. What changes can Juan's parents expect in his motor development by the time he turns seven months old?

5. If space in a child care program doesn't become available until Juan reaches seven or eight months of age, would you expect him to experience "stranger anxiety"? Explain.

6. Should Juan's parents be concerned if he doesn't show interest in pulling himself to a standing position or begin walking by his first birthday?

B. **Review Questions**

1. List three physical characteristics of the newborn.

2. List three ways in which it is possible to evaluate hearing informally in an infant who is not yet talking.

3. List three reflexes present in the newborn that should disappear by the time the infant is a year old.

4. List three perceptual-cognitive skills that appear during the first year of life.

HELPFUL WEB SITES

Brain Connection	http://www.brainconnection.com
Brainwonders	http://www.zerotothree.org
Child and Family Canada	http://www.cfc-efc.ca
Early Head Start National Resource Center	http://www.ehsnrc.org
I Am Your Child	http://www.iamyourchild.org
National Association of Child Care Resource and Referral Agencies (NACCRRA)	http://www.naccrra.org
SIDS Network	http://www.sids-network.org
U.S. Consumer Product Safety Commission	http://www.cpsc.gov

For additional child development resources, visit our Web site www.earlychilded.delmar.com

Toddlerhood

 OBJECTIVES

After reading this chapter, you should be able to:

- Describe the motor abilities of a typical one-year-old and two-year-old.
- Discuss how the speech and language skills of a two-year-old differ from those of a one-year-old.
- Explain why toddlers are often described as "picky eaters" or as having a poor appetite.
- Define and explain the concept of egocentricity.
- Provide two illustrations of the two-year-old's improved understanding of size and spatial relationships.

MEET ANNA AND JUAN

Juan's parents divorced five months ago when he was just eighteen months old. Now he and his mother, Anna, are living in a small apartment near his grandmother's house. As a single parent, Anna often feels overwhelmed by the burdens of working evenings at a local restaurant and caring for a two-year-old. Juan spends his mornings playing alone or watching television while his mother sleeps. However, he often gets into trouble, pulling objects out of kitchen drawers and bathroom cabinets because he no longer finds the few toys in his room interesting. Books, magazines, and newspapers are notably absent in their apartment. Juan's mother has little interest in reading and prefers getting her news from the television. Occasionally, Anna takes Juan to a neighborhood park to play, but most of the equipment is in poor condition and designed for older children. He usually ends up playing alone in the sand with styrofoam cups and plastic spoons he is able to find while his mother talks with friends.

Juan adores his father, Miguel, and spends every other weekend at his house. However, when he returns home his mother thinks he is unmanageable and disobedient and blames Miguel for Juan's behavior problems. They often argue about these problems in front of Juan. His grandmother is concerned about the effect his parents' divorce may be having on his development. Juan utters only two or three words that anyone can understand and shows little interest in the books his grandmother borrows from a neighbor. Increasingly, he resorts to aggression, hitting, yelling, and throwing objects whenever he is frustrated. He refuses to help dress himself, is defiant when asked to get ready for bed, and often runs the other way when his mother calls.

TWELVE TO TWENTY-FOUR MONTHS

The toddler is a dynamo, full of unlimited energy, enthusiasm, and curiosity. While the rate of growth slows considerably during this stage, important developmental changes are taking place. The toddler begins this period with the limited abilities of an infant and ends with the relatively sophisticated skills of a young child.

Improvements in motor skills enable toddlers to move about on their own, to explore, and to test their surroundings. Rapid development of speech and language contributes to more complex thinking and learning abilities. Defiance and negative responses become more commonplace near the end of this stage. Gradually, the toddler begins to assert independence as a way of gaining autonomy (a sense of self as separate and self-managed) and some degree of control over parents and teachers.

The One-Year-Old

The ability to stand upright and toddle from place to place enables one-year-olds to gain new insight about their surroundings. They become talkers and doers, stopping only for much-needed meals and bedtimes. Their curiosity mounts, their skills become increasingly advanced, and their energy level seems never-ending. One-year-olds believe that everything and everyone exists for their benefit. Eventually, this egocentricity, or self-centeredness, gives way to a greater respect for others. However, for now, the one-year-old is satisfied to declare everything "mine" and to imitate the play and actions of other children rather than join in.

1-Year-Olds

Developmental Profiles and Growth Patterns

Growth and Physical Characteristics

■ Grows at a considerably slower rate during this period.

■ Height increases approximately 2 to 3 inches (5.0–7.6 cm) per year; toddlers reach an average height of 32 to 35 inches (81.3–88.9 cm).

■ Weighs approximately 21 to 27 pounds (9.6–12.3 kg); gains 1/4 to 1/2 pound (0.13–0.25 kg) per month; weight is now approximately 3 times the child's birth weight.

■ Breathes at a rate of twenty-two to thirty respirations per minute; rate varies with emotional state and activity.

■ Heart rate (pulse) is approximately 80 to 110 per minute.

■ Head size increases slowly; grows approximately 1/2 inch (1.3 cm) every six months; anterior fontanel is nearly closed at eighteen months as bones of the skull thicken.

■ Chest circumference is larger than head circumference.

■ Teeth begin to erupt rapidly; six to ten new teeth will appear during this period.

■ Legs may still appear bowed.

■ Body shape changes; toddlers take on more adult-like appearance, but still appear top-heavy; abdomen protrudes, back is swayed.

■ Visual acuity is approximately 20/60.

Motor Development

■ Crawls skillfully and quickly.

■ Stands alone with feet spread apart, legs stiffened, and arms extended for support; Figure 5-1.

■ Gets to feet unaided.

■ Walks unassisted near the end of this period (most children); falls often; not always able to maneuver around obstacles, such as furniture or toys.

■ Uses furniture to lower self to floor; collapses backward into a sitting position or falls forward on hands and then sits.

■ Releases an object voluntarily.

■ Enjoys pushing or pulling toys while walking.

■ Picks up objects and throws them repeatedly; direction becomes more deliberate.

■ Attempts to run; has difficulty stopping and usually just drops to the floor.

■ Crawls up stairs on all fours; goes down stairs in same position.

■ Sits in a small chair.

■ Carries toys from place to place.

1-Year-Olds

Figure 5-1 Toddlers are able to stand upright with support.

■ Enjoys crayons and markers for scribbling; uses whole-arm movement.
■ Helps feed self; enjoys holding spoon (often upside down) and drinking from a glass or cup; not always accurate in getting utensils into mouth; frequent spills should be expected.
■ Helps turn pages in book.
■ Stacks two to four objects.

Perceptual-Cognitive Development

■ Enjoys object-hiding activities:
—Early in this period, the child always searches in the same location for a hidden object (if the child has watched the hiding of an object). Later, the child will search in several locations.
■ Passes toy to other hand when offered a second object (referred to as "crossing the midline"—an important neurological development).
■ Manages three to four objects by setting an object aside (on lap or floor) when presented with a new toy.

Figure 5-2 Toddlers enjoy sharing picture books with adults.

■ Puts toys in mouth less often.
■ Enjoys looking at picture books; Figure 5-2.
■ Demonstrates understanding of functional relationships (objects that belong together):
 —Puts spoon in bowl and then uses spoon as if eating.
 —Pounds wooden pegs with toy hammer.
 —Tries to make doll stand up.
■ Shows or offers toy to another person to look at.
■ Names many everyday objects.
■ Shows increasing understanding of spatial and form discrimination: puts all pegs in a pegboard; places three geometric shapes in large formboard or puzzle.
■ Places several small items (blocks, clothespins, cereal pieces) in a container or bottle and then dumps them out.
■ Tries to make mechanical objects work after watching someone else do so.
■ Responds with some facial movement, but cannot truly imitate facial expression.

1-Year-Olds

Figure 5-3 Beginning to put words together, "Me baby."

Speech and Language Development

■ Produces considerable "jargon": puts words and sounds together into speech-like (inflected) patterns; Figure 5-3.

■ Uses one word to convey an entire thought (**holophrastic speech**); meaning depends on the inflection ("me" may be used to request more cookies or desire to feed self). Later, produces two-word phrases to express a complete thought (telegraphic speech): "More cookie," "Daddy bye-bye."

■ Follows simple directions: "Give Daddy the cup."

■ Points to familiar persons, animals, and toys when asked.

■ Identifies three body parts if someone names them: "Show me your nose (toe, ear)."

■ Indicates a few desired objects and activities by name: "bye-bye," "cookie"; verbal request is often accompanied by an insistent gesture.

holophrastic speech—using a single word to express a complete thought.

Figure 5-4 Is friendly toward strangers.

■ Responds to simple questions with "yes" or "no" and appropriate head movement.
■ Produces speech that is 25 to 50 percent **intelligible** during this period.
■ Locates familiar objects on request (if child knows location of objects).
■ Acquires and uses five to fifty words; typically these are words that refer to animals, food, and toys.
■ Uses gestures, such as pointing or pulling, to direct adult attention.
■ Enjoys rhymes and songs; tries to join in.
■ Seems aware of reciprocal (back and forth) aspects of conversational exchanges; some turn-taking in other kinds of vocal exchanges, such as making and imitating sounds.

Personal-Social Development

■ Remains friendly toward others; usually less wary of strangers; Figure 5-4.
■ Helps pick up and put away toys.
■ Plays alone for short periods.
■ Enjoys being held and read to.
■ Imitates adult actions in play.
■ Enjoys adult attention; likes to know that an adult is near; gives hugs and kisses.
■ Recognizes self in mirror.
■ Enjoys the companionship of other children, but does not play cooperatively.

intelligible—language that can be understood by others.

1-Year-Olds

■ Begins to assert independence; often refuses to cooperate with daily routines that once were enjoyable; resists getting dressed, putting on shoes, eating, taking a bath; wants to try doing things without help.

■ Resorts to tantrums occasionally when things go wrong or if overly tired or frustrated.

■ Shows exceeding curiousity about people and surroundings; toddlers need to be watched carefully to prevent them from getting into unsafe situations.

Daily Routines

Twelve to Twenty-Four Months

Eating

■ Has smaller appetite; lunch is often the preferred meal.

■ Goes on occasional "food jags" (willingness to eat only a few foods); sometimes described as a picky or fussy eater; neither requires, nor wants, a large amount of food.

■ Holds food in mouth without swallowing it on occasion; this usually indicates that the child does not need or want more to eat.

■ Uses spoon with some degree of skill (if hungry and interested in eating).

■ Shows good control of cup: lifts it up, drinks from it, sets it down, holds it with one hand.

■ Helps feed self; some toddlers this age can feed themselves independently; others still need help.

Toileting, Bathing, Dressing

■ Tries to wash self; plays with washcloth and soap.

■ Helps with dressing: puts arms in sleeves, lifts feet to have socks put on. Likes to dress and undress self: takes off own shoes and stockings; often puts shirt on upside down and backward or both feet in one pant leg.

■ Lets parent or teacher know when diaper or pants are soiled or wet.

■ Begins to gain some control of bowels and bladder; complete control often not achieved until around age three.

1-Year-Olds

Sleeping

■ Falls asleep around 8 or 9 P.M.; however, will often fall asleep at dinner if nap has been missed. Sleeps through the night ten to twelve hours.

■ Experiences occasional difficulty falling asleep; overflow of energy shows itself in bouncing on the bed, calling for parent, demanding a drink or trip to the bathroom, singing, making and remaking bed—all of which seem to be ways of "winding down." A short bedtime routine promotes relaxation and helps child prepare for sleep.

■ Makes many requests at bedtime for stuffed toys, book or two, a special blanket.

Play and Social Activity

■ Develops a strong sense of property rights; "mine" is heard frequently. Sharing is difficult; hoards toys and other items.

■ Enjoys helping, but gets into trouble when left alone: smears toothpaste, tries on lipstick, empties dresser drawers.

■ Enjoys being read to; especially likes stories with repetition, such as *Jam Berry, One Duck Stuck, Five Little Monkeys,* and Dr. Seuss books; likes to talk about pictures.

■ Enjoys walks; stops frequently to look at things (rocks, bits of paper, insects); squats to examine and pick up objects; much dawdling with no real interest in getting any place in particular.

■ Plays alone (solitary play) most of the time, although beginning to show some interest in other children; lots of watching. Some occasional parallel play (play alongside, but not with another child), but no cooperative play (exception may be children who have spent considerable time in group care).

■ Seems to feel more secure and better able to settle down at bedtime if the door is left slightly ajar with light turned on in another room.

■ Continues to nap; naps too long or too late will interfere with bedtime.

■ Wakes up slowly from nap; cannot be hurried or rushed into any activity.

Learning Activities

Tips for parents and teachers:

■ Respond to the toddler's jabbering and voice inflections, both in kind (playfully) and with simple words; maintain conversational turn-taking.

■ Encourage the toddler to point to familiar objects in picture books, catalogues, and magazines; name the objects and encourage (do not insist) the toddler to imitate.

■ Hide a toy or other familiar object in an obvious place and encourage the toddler to find it (give clues as needed).

1-Year-Olds

■ Provide blocks, stacking rings, shape-sorting boxes, nesting cups; such toys promote problem solving and eye–hand coordination.

■ Allow frequent water play; the sink is always a favorite when an adult is working in the kitchen. (An old, absorbent throw rug will catch spills and drips, thus reducing the chances of slipping or falling.)

■ Put favorite toys in different parts of the room so the toddler must get to them by crawling, cruising, or walking (thus practicing motor skills).

■ Provide toys that can be pushed or pulled, a stable plastic or wooden riding toy to steer and propel with the feet; arrange safe, low places for climbing over, under, and on top of.

Developmental Alerts

Check with a health care provider or early childhood specialist if, by twenty-four months of age, the child *does not*:

■ Attempt to talk or repeat words.

■ Understand some new words.

■ Respond to simple questions with "yes" or "no."

■ Walk alone (or with very little help).

■ Exhibit a variety of emotions: anger, delight, fear.

■ Show interest in pictures.

■ Recognize self in mirror.

■ Attempt self-feeding: hold own cup to mouth and drink.

Safety Concerns

Continue to implement Safety Concerns described for the previous stages. Be aware of new safety issues as the child continues to grow and develop:

Burns (Thermal and Electrical)

■ Cover all electrical outlets with plastic caps.

■ Protect toddlers from touching hot oven doors, space heaters, hot water pipes, fireplace doors, outdoor grills, and other hot surfaces.

■ Keep cords from irons, hair curlers, and other hot electrical appliances up and out of reach.

Choking

■ Remove objects and toys with small pieces (less than 1 1/2 inch [3.75 cm] in diameter), such as coins, watch or calculator batteries, marbles, pen tops, beads, buttons, gum and hard candies, latex balloons, and plastic bags.

■ Cut foods into small pieces; insist that children eat sitting down; avoid serving foods such as popcorn, hot dogs (unless cut crosswise and in very small pieces), raw carrots, whole grapes, and hard candies.

Water Hazards

■ Eliminate sources of accessible water, such as an unsupervised wading pool, mop bucket, fish tank; purchase and use locking devices on toilet seats; *children can drown in less than 2 inches (5 cm) of water.*

Falls

■ Place safety gates across stairwells; gates can also be used to keep toddlers in rooms where they can be supervised.

■ Keep doors to outside, garage, and stairwells locked.

■ Pad sharp corners of tables and chairs.

■ Eliminate tripping hazards (e.g., electrical cords, rugs, wet spills, highly waxed floors); clear pathways of furniture and toys.

Poisons

■ Store medications (including vitamins and other nonprescription drugs), automotive and garden chemicals, and cleaning supplies in a locked cabinet (high shelves are not always safe from "climbers").

■ Check for, and remove, poisonous plants from indoor and outdoor environments (contact a local county extension agent for information).

Strangulation

■ Avoid clothing with drawstrings around the head or neck.

■ Make sure that strings on pull toys are no longer than 14 inches (35 cm) in length; supervise their use closely.

■ Fasten cords from curtains or blinds so they are high and inaccessible to children.

1-Year-Olds

The Two-Year-Old

This year can be a challenge—for the child as well as for parents and teachers. Exasperated adults typically describe a two-year-old as "impossible" (or demanding, unreasonable, contrary). However, the two-year-old's fierce determination, tantrums, and inability to accept limits are part of normal development and seldom under the child's control. The two-year-old faces demands that can be overwhelming: new skills and behaviors to be learned and remembered, learned responses to be perfected, and puzzling adult expectations with which to comply. Also, conflicting feelings of dependence and independence (autonomy) must be resolved. Is it any wonder that two-year-olds are frustrated, have difficulty making choices, and say no even to things they really want?

While this year of transition can be somewhat trying for all, many good things also happen. Two-year-olds are noted for their frequent and spontaneous outbursts of laughter and affection. New skills are learned quickly as a result of determined interest in self-discovery and independence. Gradually, the two-year-old begins to function more ably and amiably as newly acquired skills and earlier learning are consolidated.

Developmental Profiles and Growth Patterns

Growth and Physical Characteristics

■ Gains an average of 2 to 2.5 pounds (0.9–1.1 kg) per year; weighs approximately 26 to 32 pounds (11.8–14.5 kg) or about 4 times the weight at birth.

■ Grows approximately 3 to 5 inches (7.6–12.7 cm) per year; average height is 34 to 38 inches (86.3–96.5 cm) tall.

■ Assumes a more erect posture; abdomen still large and protruding, back swayed, because abdominal muscles are not yet fully developed.

■ Respirations are slow and regular (approximately twenty to thirty-five breaths per minute).

■ Body temperature continues to fluctuate with activity, emotional state, and environment.

■ Brain reaches about 80 percent of its adult size.

■ Eruption of teeth is nearly complete; second molars appear, for a total of twenty deciduous or "baby" teeth.

Motor Development

■ Walks with a more erect, heel-to-toe pattern; able to maneuver around obstacles in pathway.

Figure 5-5 Tries hard to balance on one foot.

■ Runs with greater confidence; has fewer falls.
■ Squats for long periods while playing.
■ Climbs stairs unassisted (but not with alternating feet).
■ Balances on one foot (for a few moments), jumps up and down, but may fall; Figure 5-5.
■ Begins to achieve toilet training during this year (depending on child's physical and neurological development) although accidents should still be expected; the child will indicate readiness for toilet training.
■ Throws large ball underhand without losing balance.
■ Holds cup or glass (be sure it is unbreakable) in one hand.
■ Unbuttons large buttons; unzips large zippers.
■ Opens doors by turning doorknobs.
■ Grasps large crayon with fist; scribbles enthusiastically on large piece of paper.
■ Climbs up on chair, turns around and sits down.
■ Enjoys pouring and filling activities—sand, water, styrofoam peanuts.
■ Stacks four to six objects on top of one another.
■ Uses feet to propel wheeled riding toys.

Perceptual-Cognitive Development

■ Exhibits eye–hand movements that are better coordinated; can put objects together, take them apart; fit large pegs into pegboard.

■ Begins to use objects for purposes other than intended (may push a block around as a boat).

■ Completes simple classification tasks based on one dimension (separates toy dinosaurs from toy cars).

■ Stares for long moments; seems fascinated by, or engrossed in, figuring out a situation: where the tennis ball has rolled, where the dog has gone, what has caused a particular noise.

■ Attends to self-selected activities for longer periods of time.

■ Shows discovery of cause and effect: squeezing the cat makes her scratch.

■ Knows where familiar persons should be; notes their absence; finds a hidden object by looking in last hiding place first.

■ Names objects in picture books; may pretend to pick something off the page and taste or smell it.

■ Recognizes and expresses pain and its location.

Speech and Language Development

■ Enjoys being read to if allowed to participate by pointing, making relevant noises, turning pages.

■ Realizes that language is effective for getting others to respond to needs and preferences.

■ Uses 50 to 300 different words; vocabulary continuously increasing.

■ Has broken the **linguistic code**; in other words, much of a two-year-old's talk has meaning to him or her.

■ Understands significantly more language than is able to communicate verbally; most two-year-olds' receptive language is more developed than their expressive language.

■ Utters three- and four-word statements; uses conventional word order to form more complete sentences.

■ Refers to self as "me" or sometimes "I" rather than by name: "Me go bye-bye"; has no trouble verbalizing "mine."

■ Expresses negative statements by tacking on a negative word such as "no" or "not": "Not more milk."

■ Asks repeatedly, "What's that?"

---

linguistic code—verbal expression that has meaning to the child.

Figure 5-6 Often shows concern for a hurt friend.

- Uses some plurals; tells about objects and events not immediately present (this is both a cognitive and a linguistic advance).
- Experiences occasional stammering and other common **dysfluencies.**
- Produces speech that is as much as 65 to 70 percent intelligible.

Personal-Social Development

- Shows signs of empathy and caring: comforts another child who is hurt or frightened; sometimes is overly affectionate in offering hugs and kisses to children; Figure 5-6.
- Continues to use physical aggression if frustrated or angry (for some children, this is more exaggerated than for others); physical aggression usually lessens as verbal skills improve.
- Expresses frustration through temper tantrums; frequency of tantrums often peaks during this year; cannot be reasoned with while tantrum is in progress.
- Finds it difficult to wait or take turns; often impatient.
- Enjoys "helping" with household chores; imitates everyday activities: may try to toilet a stuffed animal, feed a doll.
- Orders parents and teachers around; is "bossy"; makes demands and expects immediate compliance from adults.
- Watches and imitates the play of other children, but seldom joins in; content to play alone; Figure 5-7.

---

dysfluency—repetition of whole words or phrases uttered without frustration and often at the beginning of a statement; "Let's go, let's go get some cookies."

Figure 5-7 Still prefers to play alone.

■ Offers toys to other children, but is usually possessive of playthings; still tends to hoard toys.

■ Finds it difficult to make choices; wants it both ways.

■ Shows much defiance; shouting "no" becomes almost automatic.

■ Wants everything "just so"; is quite ritualistic; expects routines to be carried out exactly as before and belongings placed "where they belong."

Daily Routines

Two-Year-Olds

Eating

■ Has fair appetite; interest in food fluctuates with periods of growth; lunch is often the preferred meal.

■ Sometimes described as a picky or fussy eater; often has strong likes and dislikes (which should be respected); may go on food jags (only eating certain foods, such as peanut butter and jelly sandwiches, macaroni and cheese).

■ Likes simple, "recognizable" foods; dislikes mixtures; wants foods served in familiar ways.

■ Needs between-meal snacks; should be of good nutritive value, with "junk" foods limited.

■ Feeds self with increasing skill, but may be "too tired" or disinterested at times.

■ Has good control of cup or glass, although spills happen often.

■ Learns table manners by imitating adults and older children.

Toileting, Bathing, Dressing

■ Enjoys bath if allowed ample playtime (*must never be left alone*); may object to being washed; tries to wash by self; Figure 5-8.

■ Dislikes, even resists, having hair washed.

■ Tries to help when being dressed; needs simple, manageable clothing; can usually undress self.

■ Shows signs of readiness for bowel training (some children may have already mastered bowel control).

■ Stays dry for longer periods of time (one sign of readiness for toilet training); other signs include interest in watching others use toilet, holding a doll or stuffed animal over toilet, clutching self, willingness to sit on potty for a few moments, expressing discomfort about being wet or soiled.

Sleeping

■ Sleeps between nine and twelve hours at nighttime.

■ Still requires afternoon nap; needs time to wake up slowly.

■ Resists going to bed; however, usually complies if given ample warning and can depend on a familiar bedtime routine (story, talk time, special toy).

■ Takes awhile to fall asleep, especially if overly tired; may sing, talk to self, bounce on bed, call for parents, make and remake the bed (again, ways of "winding down").

Figure 5-8 "Look daddy, all clean!"

Play and Social Activity

■ Enjoys dressing up and imitating family activities: wearing Father's hat makes a child a "daddy."

■ Likes to be around other children, but does not play well with them: observes them intently, imitating their actions (parallel play).

■ Displays extreme negativism toward parents and caregivers—an early step toward establishing independence.

■ Pretends to have an imaginary friend as a constant companion.

■ Explores everything in the environment, including other children; may shove or push other children as if to test their reaction.

Learning Activities

Tips for parents and teachers:

■ Share games, such as large lotto and picture dominoes, that are based on matching colors, animals, facial expressions, and everyday objects.

■ Offer manipulative materials to foster problem solving and eye–hand coordination: large beads for stringing, brightly colored cubes, puzzle boxes, large, plastic interlocking bricks.

- Provide toy replicas of farm and zoo animals, families, cars, trucks, and planes for sorting and imaginative play.

- Read to the child regularly; provide colorful picture books for naming objects and describing everyday events; use simple, illustrated storybooks (one line per page) so the child can learn to tell the story.

- Share nursery rhymes, simple finger plays, and action songs; respond to, imitate, and make up simple games based on the child's spontaneous rhyming or chanting.

- Set out (and keep a close eye on) washable paints, markers, chalk, large crayons, and large paper for artistic expression.

- Help with make-believe activities; for example: save empty cereal boxes, plastic juice containers with intact labels for playing store.

- Provide wagons; large trucks and cars that can be loaded, pushed, or sat on; doll carriage or stroller; a rocking boat; bean bags and rings for tossing.

Developmental Alerts

Check with a health care provider or early childhood specialist if, by the third birthday, the child *does not*:

- Eat a fairly well-rounded diet, even though amounts are limited.

- Walk confidently with few stumbles or falls; climb steps with help.

- Avoid bumping into objects.

- Carry out simple, two-step directions: "Come to Daddy and bring your book"; express desires; ask questions.

- Point to and name familiar objects; use two- or three-word sentences.

- Enjoy being read to.

- Show interest in playing with other children: watching, perhaps imitating.

- Indicate a beginning interest in toilet training.

- Sort familiar objects according to a single characteristic, such as type, color, or size.

Safety Concerns

Continue to implement Safety Concerns described for the previous stages. Be aware of new safety issues as the child continues to grow and develop:

Burns

■ Set temperature of hot water heater no higher than 120°F.

■ Purchase and use protective devices on bathtub faucets.

■ Keep hot liquids (e.g., coffee cups, kettles) out of reach.

Choking

■ Continue to cut food into small pieces; insist that children eat sitting down; avoid popcorn, hot dogs (unless cut crosswise in small pieces), raw carrots, whole grapes, and hard candies.

Water

■ Supervise any source of accessible water (e.g., wading pool, fish tank, garden pond or fountain, bathtub); *children can drown in less than 2 inches (5 cm) of water. Never leave children unattended.*

Play Environments

■ Securely fasten bookcases, filing cabinets, dressers, and shelves to the wall to prevent them from tipping over.

■ Place toys on lower shelves so they are accessible.

■ Keep doors to the outside and stairwells locked.

Poisons

■ Store all medicines (including vitamins and other nonprescription drugs), automotive and garden chemicals, and cleaning supplies in a locked cabinet (high shelves are not safe from "climbers").

■ Check for, and remove, poisonous plants from indoor and outdoor environments (contact a local county extension agent for information).

Strangulation

■ Avoid "dress-up" clothing that could become tangled around a child's neck (e.g., neck ties, drawstrings).

SUMMARY

Toddlers continue to undergo important physical changes, although their rate of growth begins to slow. Improving motor skills tend to outpace toddlers' cognitive development—their understanding of cause and effect, judgment of size and distance, and functionality—thus, placing them at high risk of accidental injury. Although vocabulary (expressive language) may be limited, toddlers' understanding of language (receptive language) is generally more advanced. However, dramatic increases in the number of words and their usage occur between the first and second birthdays. Toddlers enjoy being read to, singing, repeating simple words, and imitating adult behaviors. Curiosity often gets them into trouble as they experiment with everyday objects, explore every nook and cranny, and attempt to take things apart. Efforts to achieve autonomy often result in bouts of defiance and temper tantrums.

KEY TERMS

dysfluency   intelligible

holophrastic speech   linguistic code

APPLY YOUR KNOWLEDGE

A. Apply What You Have Learned

Reread the developmental sketch about Juan and his parents at the beginning of the chapter. How might you answer the following questions?

1. Should Juan's grandmother be concerned about his language development?

2. What factors in Juan's home environment may be limiting his language development?

3. What suggestions could you offer to Anna for encouraging Juan's language development, taking into consideration the family's financial situation?

4. If you were asked to evaluate Juan's behavior, would you consider his displays of anger and aggression to be typical or atypical of a toddler? Explain.

5. From a developmental perspective, is it appropriate for Juan's mother to punish him for getting into the kitchen cabinets and pulling items out of drawers?

6. Because Anna sleeps in the morning while Juan is playing, what special precautions should she take in their apartment to ensure his safety?

B. Review Questions

1. Identify two motor skills that one- and two-year-olds typically acquire.

2. List three developmentally appropriate activities for a two-year-old (based on perceptual-cognitive and motor skills).

3. List three ways in which a one-year-old may begin to assert independence.

4. What are some things parents and teachers can do to help two-year-olds settle down for sleep?

5. Describe three activities designed to help two-year-olds learn about the concept of size.

 HELPFUL WEB SITES

American Speech, Language, & Hearing Association	http://www.asha.org
Early Head Start National Resource Center	http://www.ehsnrc.org
National Association for the Education of Young Children (NAEYC)	http://www.naeyc.org
Parent Information	http://www.parentsoup.com
Your Child's Health	http://www.yourchildshealth.echn.ca
Zero To Three; National Center for Infants, Toddlers, and Families	http://www.zerotothree.org

 **For additional child development resources, visit our Web site www.earlychilded.delmar.com**

Chapter 6

Early Childhood: Three-, Four-, and Five-Year-Olds

OBJECTIVES

After reading this chapter, you should be able to:

- Contrast the major developmental characteristics of typical three-, four-, and five-year-olds with those of toddlers.
- Describe the food preferences, eating habits, and calorie needs of typical three-year-olds, four-year-olds, and five-year-olds.
- Discuss the preschoolers' need for adult attention and then trace the ways these needs change with increasing independence.
- Contrast the average three-year-old's language skills with those of an average five-year-old.
- List a minimum of five things that adults can do to promote cognitive develop and support emerging literacy with three-, four-, and five-year-olds.

MEET FOUR-YEAR-OLD JUAN AND HIS MOTHER

Anna's interest in resuming her education was sparked after she attended a recruiting program sponsored by the local community college. When Anna discovered there was space for Juan at the child care center on campus, she was even more determined. Anna knows that Juan's language and social development are delayed, and believes he will benefit from having more opportunities to interact with children his own age.

Each morning, Anna drops Juan off at the child care center while she attends classes and works in the school cafeteria. However, Juan isn't sure he likes his new school. He prefers to play alone, seldom stays involved in any activity for more than a few minutes, and insists on carrying his blanket wherever he goes.

Despite her busy schedule, Anna sets aside time in the evenings to play with Juan. They talk about things Juan has done in school that day and sometimes work on art projects. Before Juan heads to bed, they always sit quietly and read several books together. Anna is becoming increasingly confident in her ability to facilitate Juan's development ever since attending a parent education class at the college. She now realizes how simple, everyday things she does with her son help him to learn. Anna thinks she would enjoy working with children and is seriously considering becoming an early education teacher.

THREE-, FOUR, AND FIVE-YEAR OLDS

Typically, three-, four-, and five-year-olds are full of energy, eagerness, and curiosity. They seem to be constantly on the move as they engross themselves totally in whatever captures their interest at the moment. During these years, motor skills are being perfected. Creativity and imagination come into everything, from dramatic play to artwork to storytelling. Vocabulary and intellectual skills expand rapidly, allowing the child to express ideas, solve problems, and plan ahead. Preschool children strongly believe in their own opinions. At the same time, they are developing some sense of the needs of others and some degree of control over their own behavior. They strive for independence, yet need reassurance that an adult is available to give assistance, to comfort, or to rescue, if need be.

The Three-Year-Old

Three-year-olds tend to be more peaceful, relaxed, and cooperative. Conflicts with adults, growing out of the two-year-old's struggle for independence, are fewer and less intense. In fact, many three-year-olds are willing to abide by parents' and caregivers' directions much of the time. They are able to delay their own gratification longer; that is, they have less need to have what they want "right now." They take obvious delight in themselves and life in general and show an irrepressible urge to find out all about everything in the world around them.

Developmental Profiles and Growth Patterns

Growth and Physical Characteristics

■ Growth is steady although slower than in the first two years.

■ Height increases 2 to 3 inches (5–7.6 cm) per year; average height is 38 to 40 inches (96.5–101.6 cm), nearly double the child's birth length.

■ Adult height can be predicted from measurements of height at three years of age; males are approximately 53 percent of their adult height and females, 57 percent.

■ Gains an average of 3 to 5 pounds (1.4–2.3 kg) per year; weight averages 30 to 38 pounds (13.6–17.2 kg).

■ Heart rate (pulse) averages 90 to 110 beats per minute.

■ Respiratory rate is twenty to thirty, depending on activity level; child continues to breathe abdominally.

■ Temperature averages 96°F to 99.4°F (35.5°C–37.4°C); is affected by exertion, illness, and stress.

■ Legs grow more rapidly than growth of arms, giving the three-year-old a taller, thinner, adult-like appearance.

■ Circumference of head and chest is equal; head size is in better proportion to the body.

■ Neck appears to lengthen as "baby fat" disappears.

■ Posture is more erect; abdomen no longer protrudes.

■ Still appears slightly knock-kneed.

■ Has a full set of "baby" teeth.

■ Needs to consume approximately 1,500 calories daily.

■ Visual acuity is approximately 20/40 using the Snellen E chart.

Motor Development

■ Walks up and down stairs unassisted, using alternating feet; may jump from bottom step, landing on both feet; Figure 6-1.

■ Balances momentarily on one foot.

■ Kicks a large ball.

■ Feeds self; needs minimal assistance.

■ Jumps in place.

■ Pedals a small tricycle or Bigwheel.

■ Catches a large bounced ball with both arms extended.

■ Enjoys swinging on a swing (not too high or too fast).

tripod grasp—hand position, whereby an object, such as a pencil, is held between the thumb, first, and second fingers.

3-Year-Olds

Figure 6-1 Walks up and down stairs using alternating feet.

Figure 6-2 Holds marker in tripod grasp.

■ Shows improved control of crayons or makers; uses vertical, horizontal, and circular strokes.
■ Holds crayon or marker between first two fingers and thumb (**tripod grasp**), not in a fist as earlier; Figure 6-2.
■ Turns pages of a book one at a time.
■ Enjoys building with blocks.
■ Builds a tower of eight or more blocks; Figure 6-3.
■ Enjoys playing with clay; pounds, rolls, and squeezes it.
■ Begins to show **hand dominance**.
■ Carries a container of liquid, such as a cup of milk or bowl of water, without much spilling; pours liquid from pitcher into another container.
■ Manipulates large buttons and zippers on clothing.
■ Washes and dries hands; brushes own teeth, but not thoroughly.
■ Achieves complete bladder control, for the most part, during this time.

hand dominance—preference for using one hand over the other; most individuals are said to be either right- or left-handed.

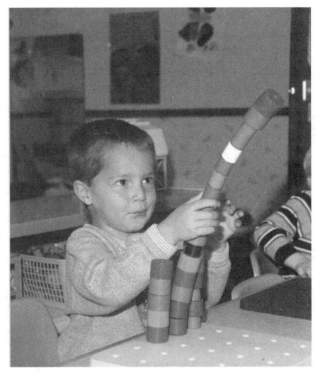

Figure 6-3 Builds tower of eight or more blocks.

Perceptual-Cognitive Development

■ Listens attentively to age-appropriate stories.

■ Makes relevant comments during stories, especially those that relate to home and family events.

■ Likes to look at books and may pretend to "read" to others or explain pictures; Figure 6-4.

■ Enjoys stories with riddles, guessing, and suspense.

■ Points with a fair degree of accuracy to correct pictures when given sound-alike words: *keys–cheese; fish–dish; mouse–mouth*.

■ Plays realistically:

—Feeds doll, puts down for nap, covers it.

—Hooks truck and trailer together, loads truck, drives away making motor noises.

■ Places eight to ten pegs in pegboard, or six round and six square blocks in formboard.

■ Attempts to draw; imperfectly copies circles, squares, and some letters.

■ Understands triangle, circle, square; can point to requested shape.

Figure 6-4 May "read" to others or explain pictures.

■ Sorts objects logically on the basis of one dimension, such as color, shape, or size; usually chooses color or size as basis for classification: all red beads in one pile, green beads in another.

■ Shows understanding of basic size–shape comparisons much of the time; will indicate which is bigger when shown a tennis ball and a golf ball; also understands "smaller of the two."

■ Names and matches, at a minimum, primary colors: red, yellow, blue.

■ Arranges cubes in horizontal line; also positions cubes to form a bridge.

■ Counts objects out loud; Figure 6-5.

■ Points to picture that has "more": cars, planes, or kittens.

■ Shows some understanding of duration of time by using phrases such as "all the time," "all day," "for two days"; some confusion remains: "I didn't take a nap tomorrow."

Speech and Language Development

■ Talks about objects, events, and people not present: "Jerry has a pool in his yard."

■ Talks about the actions of others: "Daddy's mowing the grass."

■ Adds information to what has just been said: "Yeah, and then he grabbed it back."

■ Answers simple questions appropriately.

Figure 6-5 Counts out loud: 1, 2, 3, 4. . . .

■ Asks increasing numbers of questions, particularly about location and identity of objects and people.

■ Uses an increasing number of speech forms that keep conversation going: "What did he do next?" "How come she hid?"

■ Calls attention to self, objects, or events in the environment: "Watch my helicopter fly."

■ Promotes the behavior of others: "Let's jump in the water. You go first."

■ Joins in social interaction rituals: "Hi," "Bye," "Please."

■ Comments about objects and ongoing events: "There's a house"; "The tractor's pushing a boat."

■ Vocabulary has increased; now uses 300 to 1,000 words.

■ Recites nursery rhymes, sings songs.

■ Uses understandable speech most of the time.

■ Produces expanded noun phrases: "big, brown dog."

■ Produces verbs with "ing" endings; uses "-s" to indicate more than one; often puts "-s" on already pluralized forms: geeses, mices.

■ Indicates negatives by inserting "no" or "not" before a simple noun or verb phrase: "Not baby."

■ Answers "What are you doing?" "What is this?" and "Where?" questions dealing with familiar objects and events.

Figure 6-6 Engages in make-believe.

Personal-Social Development

◼ Seems to understand taking turns, but not always willing to do so.

◼ Laughs frequently; is friendly and eager to please.

◼ Has occasional nightmares and fears the dark, monsters, or fire.

◼ Joins in simple games and group activities, sometimes hesitantly.

◼ Talks to self often.

◼ Uses objects symbolically in play: block of wood may be a truck, a ramp, a bat.

◼ Observes other children playing; may join in for a short time; often plays parallel to other children.

◼ Defends toys and possessions; may become aggressive at times by grabbing a toy, hitting another child, hiding toys.

◼ Engages in make-believe play alone and with other children; Figure 6-6.

◼ Shows affection toward children who are younger or children who get hurt.

◼ Sits and listens to stories up to ten minutes at a time; does not bother other children listening to story and resents being bothered.

◼ May continue to have a special blanket, stuffed animal, or toy for comfort.

Daily Routines

Three-Year-Olds

Eating

- Prefers small servings; appetite is fair. Dislikes many cooked vegetables; eats almost everything else; should never be forced to eat.
- Feeds self independently if hungry. Uses spoon in semi-adult fashion; may spear with fork.
- Dawdles over food, or plays with it, when not hungry.
- Pours milk and juice with fewer spills; serves individual portions from a serving dish with some prompts ("Fill it up to the line"; "Take only two spoonsful").
- Drinks a great deal of milk. (Be sure child does not fill up on milk to the exclusion of other needed foods.)

Toileting, Bathing, Dressing

- Does a fair job of washing self in bathtub; often resists getting out of tub.
- Takes care of own toilet needs during the daytime (boys, especially, may continue to have wet-pants days).
- Some children sleep through the night without wetting the bed; others are in transition—they may stay dry at night for days or weeks, then go back to night-wetting for a period.
- Manages undressing better than dressing, although is capable of putting on some articles of clothing.
- Manipulates zippers, large buttons, and snaps with improving ability.

Sleeping

- Sleeps ten to twelve hours most nights, waking up about 7 or 8 A.M.; some children are awake much earlier.
- Begins to give up afternoon naps; however, continues to benefit from a midday quiet time.
- Prepares for bed independently most of the time; has given up many earlier bedtime rituals; still needs a bedtime story or song and tucking-in.
- Has dreams that may cause the child to awaken.
- Sometimes wanders at night; quiet firmness may be needed in returning child to own bed.

Play and Social Activity

■ Wants to be included in everything; the "me too" age.

■ Joins in spontaneous group play for short periods; very social; beginning to play cooperatively.

■ Argues or quarrels with other children occasionally; adults should allow children to settle their own disagreements unless physical harm is threatened.

■ Loves dress-up, dramatic play that involves everyday work activities. Some children still exhibit strong **gender** and role stereotypes: "Boys can't be nurses."

■ Responds well to options rather than commands: "Do you want to put your pajamas on before or after the story?"

■ Finds sharing still difficult, but seems to understand the concept.

Learning Activities

Tips for parents and teachers:

■ Allow the child to create new uses for everyday household items and discards: blanket over a table to make a cave; utensils for pretend cooking; discarded mail for playing mail carrier; hose with trickle of water for washing tricycle or wagon; oil can for servicing the vehicles.

■ Provide somewhat more complex manipulative materials: parquetry blocks; pegboards with multicolored pegs; various items to count, sort, and match; construction sets with medium-size, interlocking pieces.

■ Offer art and craft materials that encourage experimentation: crayons, washable markers, chalk, modeling clay, round-tipped scissors, papers, glue, paints, and large brushes (supervision required).

■ Keep on hand a plentiful supply of books about animals, families, everyday events, alphabet and counting activities, poems and rhymes; continue daily reading sessions.

■ Make regular trips to the library; allow plenty of time for child to make own book selections.

■ Provide wheeled riding toys that build eye–hand–foot dexterity through steering and maneuvering; also wheelbarrow and garden tools, doll stroller, shopping cart.

gender—reference to being either male or female.

■ Go for walks with the child, *at the child's pace*; allow ample time for child to explore, observe, and collect rocks, leaves, seed pods; name and talk about things along the way.

Developmental Alerts

Check with a health care provider or early childhood specialist if, by the fourth birthday, the child *does not*:

■ Have intelligible speech most of the time; have children's hearing checked if there is any reason for concern.

■ Understand and follow simple commands and directions.

■ State own name and age.

■ Enjoy playing near or with other children.

■ Use three- to four-word sentences.

■ Ask questions.

■ Stay with an activity for three or four minutes; play alone several minutes at a time.

■ Jump in place without falling.

■ Balance on one foot, at least briefly.

■ Help with dressing self.

Safety Concerns

Continue to implement Safety Concerns described for the previous stages. Be aware of new safety issues as the child continues to grow and develop:

Burns

■ Keep hot items out of children's reach.

■ Place lighted candles, matches, cigarette lighters where they are inaccessible.

■ Monitor children carefully when grills or fireplaces are lit.

Choking

■ Avoid foods likely to cause choking, such as popcorn, nuts, raw carrots, hard candies, and grapes.

■ Cut food into small pieces and insist that children sit quietly when eating.

■ Supervise children closely when they are eating items with sticks, such as a lollipop or popsicle.

Drowning

■ Continue to supervise children closely when around any source of water.

■ Always empty wading pools.

■ Fence in permanent pools; use pool alarm; keep gates closed and riding toys away from pool area.

■ Know CPR!

Falls

■ Provide sturdy, flat-soled shoes to prevent twisted ankles and tripping. Falls when climbing are also more likely if shoes have hard or slippery soles.

Poisons

■ Avoid use of pesticides and chemicals on grass where children play; residues can get on hands and in sand boxes.

Traffic

■ Insist on holding child's hand when walking in parking lots or crossing streets.

■ Always buckle child securely into appropriate car seat.

The Four-Year-Old

Tireless bundles of energy, brimful of ideas, overflowing with chatter and activity—these are the characteristics typical of most four-year-olds. Bouts of stubbornness and arguments between child and parent or caregiver may be frequent. Children often test limits, practice self-confidence, and firm up a growing need for independence. Many are loud, boisterous, even belligerent; they try adults' patience with silly talk and silly jokes, constant chatter, and endless questions. At the same time, they have many lovable qualities. They are enthusiastic, try hard to be helpful, have lively imaginations, and can plan ahead to some extent: "When we get home, I'll make you a picture."

Developmental Profiles and Growth Patterns

Growth and Physical Characteristics

- Gains approximately 4 to 5 pounds (1.8–2.3 kg) per year; weighs an average of 32 to 40 pounds (14.5–18.2 kg).
- Grows 2 to 2.5 inches (5.0–6.4 cm) in height per year; is approximately 40 to 45 inches (101.6–114 cm) tall.
- Heart rate (pulse) averages 90 to 110 beats per minute.
- Respiratory rate ranges from twenty to thirty, varying with activity and emotional state.
- Body temperature ranges from 98°F to 99.4°F (36.6°C–37.4°C).
- Head circumference is usually not measured after age three.
- Requires approximately 1,700 calories daily.
- Hearing acuity can be assessed by child's correct usage of sounds and language; also, by the child's appropriate responses to questions and instructions.
- Visual acuity is 20/30 as measured on the Snellen E chart.

Motor Development

- Walks a straight line (tape or chalkline on the floor).
- Hops on one foot.
- Pedals and steers a wheeled toy with confidence; turns corners, avoids obstacles and oncoming "traffic."
- Climbs ladders, trees, playground equipment; Figure 6-7.
- Jumps over objects 5 or 6 inches (12.5 to 15 cm) high; lands with both feet together.
- Runs, starts, stops, and moves around obstacles with ease.
- Throws a ball overhand; distance and aim improving.
- Builds a tower with ten or more blocks.
- Forms shapes and objects out of clay: cookies, snakes, simple animals.
- Reproduces some shapes and letters.
- Holds a crayon or marker using a tripod grasp.
- Paints and draws with purpose; may have an idea in mind, but often has trouble implementing it so calls the creation something else.
- Becomes more accurate at hitting nails and pegs with hammer.
- Threads small wooden beads on a string.

Perceptual-Cognitive Development

- Stacks at least five graduated cubes from largest to smallest; builds a pyramid of six blocks.

Figure 6-7 Enjoys climbing.

■ Indicates if paired words sound the same or different: *sheet–feet, ball–wall.*
■ Names eighteen to twenty uppercase letters near the end of this year; some children may be able to print several and write own name; may recognize some printed words (especially those that have a special meaning for the child).
■ A few children are beginning to read simple books, such as alphabet books with only a few words per page and many pictures.
■ Likes stories about how things grow and operate.
■ Delights in wordplay, creating silly language.
■ Understands the concepts of "tallest," "biggest," "same," and "more"; selects the picture that has the "most houses" or the "biggest dogs."
■ Rote counts to 20 or more.
■ Understands the sequence of daily events: "When we get up in the morning, we get dressed, have breakfast, brush our teeth, and go to school."
■ Recognizes and identifies missing puzzle parts (of person, car, animal) when looking at the picture.

Figure 6-8 Answers questions appropriately about "how many."

Speech and Language Development

- Uses the prepositions "on," "in," and "under."
- Uses possessives consistently: "hers," "theirs," "baby's."
- Answers "Whose?" "Who?" "Why?" and "How many?"; Figure 6-8.
- Produces elaborate sentence structures: "The cat ran under the house before I could see what color it was."
- Uses almost entirely intelligible speech.
- Begins to correctly use the past tense of verbs: "Mommy closed the door," "Daddy went to work."
- Refers to activities, events, objects, and people that are not present.
- Changes tone of voice and sentence structure to adapt to listener's level of understanding: To baby brother, "Milk gone?" To Mother, "Did the baby drink all of his milk?"
- States first and last name, gender, siblings' names, and sometimes home telephone number.

Figure 6-9 Begins to have a "best" friend.

■ Answers appropriately when asked what to do if tired, cold, or hungry.
■ Recites and sings simple songs and rhymes.

Personal-Social Development

■ Is outgoing and friendly; overly enthusiastic at times.
■ Changes moods rapidly and unpredictably; may laugh one minute, cry the next; often throws tantrum over minor frustrations (a block structure that will not balance); sulk over being left out.
■ Holds conversations and shares strong emotions with imaginary playmates or companions; having an invisible friend is fairly common.
■ Boasts, exaggerates, and "bends" the truth with made-up stories or claims of boldness; tests the limits with "bathroom" talk.
■ Cooperates with others; participates in group activities.
■ Shows pride in accomplishments; seeks frequent adult approval.
■ Tattles on other children; often appears selfish; not always able to take turns or to understand taking turns under some conditions.
■ Insists on trying to do things independently, but may get so frustrated as to verge on tantrums when problems arise: paint that drips, paper airplane that will not fold right.
■ Enjoys role-playing and make-believe activities.

- Relies (most of the time) on verbal rather than physical aggression; may yell angrily rather than hit to make a point; threatens: "You can't come to my birthday party."
- Uses name-calling and taunting as ways of excluding other children.
- Establishes close relationships with playmates; beginning to have "best" friends; Figure 6-9.

Daily Routines

Four-Year-Olds

Eating

- Appetite fluctuates from very good to fair.
- May develop dislikes of certain foods and refuse them to the point of tears if pushed (such pressure can cause serious adult–child conflict).
- Able to use all eating utensils; quite skilled at spreading jelly or butter or cutting soft foods such as bread.
- Eating and talking get in each other's way; talking usually takes precedence over eating.
- Likes to help in the preparation of a meal; dumping premeasured ingredients, washing vegetables, setting the table.

Toileting, Bathing, Dressing

- Takes care of own toileting needs; often demands privacy in the bathroom.
- Does an acceptable job of bathing and brushing teeth, but should receive assistance (or subtle inspection) from adults regularly.
- Dresses self; can lace shoes, button buttons, buckle belts. Gets frustrated if problems arise in getting dressed while stubbornly refusing much-needed adult help.
- Can help sort and fold own clean clothes, put clothes away, hang up towels, straighten room; easily distracted, however.

Sleeping

- Averages ten to twelve hours of sleep at night; may still take an afternoon nap.
- Bedtime usually not a problem if cues, rather than orders, signal the time: when the story is finished, when the clock hands are in a certain position.
- Some children fear the dark, but usually a light left on in the hall is all that is needed.
- Getting up to use the toilet may require helping the child settle down for sleep again.

4-Year-Olds

Play and Social Activities

■ Playmates are important; plays cooperatively some of the time; may be "bossy."
■ Takes turns; shares (most of the time); wants to be with children every waking moment.
■ Needs (and seeks out) adult approval and attention; may comment, "Look what I did."
■ Understands and needs limits (but not too constraining); will abide by rules most of the time.
■ Brags about possessions; shows off; boasts about family members.

Learning Activities

Tips for parents and teachers:

■ Join in simple board and card games (picture lotto, Candyland) that depend on chance, not strategy; emphasis should be on playing, not winning. (Learning to be a "good sport" does not come until much later.)

■ Provide puzzles with five to twenty pieces (number depends on the child), counting and alphabet games, matching games, such as more detailed lotto.

■ Offer various kinds of simple scientific and math materials: ruler, compass, magnifying glass, simple scales; activities, such as collecting leaves, growing worms, sprouting seeds.

■ Appreciate (and sometimes join in) the child's spontaneous rhyming, chanting, silly name-calling, jokes, riddles.

■ Continue daily read-aloud times; encourage the child to supply words or phrases, to guess *what comes next,* to retell the story (or parts of it); introduce the idea of looking things up in a simple picture dictionary or encyclopedia; go to the library regularly, allowing the child ample time to choose books.

■ Encourage all kinds of vigorous outdoor activity; water play in sprinkler or plastic pool (*pool requires adult presence*); offer unpressured swimming, tumbling, or dancing lessons; provide balls for kicking and throwing.

Developmental Alerts

Check with a health care provider or early childhood specialist if, by the fifth birthday, the child *does not:*

■ State own name in full.

- Recognize simple shapes: circle, square, triangle.
- Catch a large ball when bounced (have child's vision checked).
- Speak so as to be understood by strangers (have child's hearing checked).
- Have good control of posture and movement.
- Hop on one foot.
- Appear interested in, and responsive to, surroundings.
- Respond to statements without constantly asking to have them repeated.
- Dress self with minimal adult assistance; manage buttons, zippers.
- Take care of own toilet needs; have good bowel and bladder control with infrequent accidents.

 ## *Safety Concerns*

Continue to implement Safety Concerns described for the previous stages. Be aware of new safety issues as the child continues to grow and develop:

Burns

- Teach children the dangers of fire.
- Make sure smoke and carbon monoxide detectors are operational. Use cooking opportunities to help children learn good safety practices.

Dangerous Objects

- Keep all chemicals, cleaning supplies, personal care products, medications, guns, and dangerous tools in locked storage; curiosity peaks during this stage.

Falls

- Always insist that children wear bike helmet and pads when biking, skating, or skateboarding.
- Rethink the use of trampolines; many children sustain serious injuries, including head and spinal cord injuries.

Personal Safety

- Teach children their full name, telephone number, and what to do if they become lost. Increased independence may cause children to wander too far from parents/teachers.

4-Year-Olds

Toys

■ When purchasing toys, evaluate their safety (e.g., rounded edges, not easily broken, no protruding wires, no electrical connections, nontoxic and non-flammable materials).

■ Avoid toys with small parts if there are younger children in the home or child care setting.

Suffocation

■ Remove doors from unused freezer or refrigerator and dispose of the appliance.

■ Select toy boxes with removable lids or use open containers to prevent children from being trapped by a fallen top.

The Five-Year-Old

More in control of themselves, both physically and emotionally, most five-year-olds are in a period of relative calm. The child is friendly and outgoing much of the time and is becoming self-confident and reliable. The world is expanding beyond home and family and child care center. Friendships and group activities are of major importance.

Constant practice and mastery of skills in all areas of development is the major focus of the five-year-old. However, this quest for mastery, coupled with a high energy level and robust self-confidence, can lead to mishaps. Eagerness to do and explore often interferes with the ability to foresee danger or potentially disastrous consequences. Therefore, the child's safety and the prevention of accidents must be a major concern of parents and caregivers. At the same time, adults' concerns must be handled in ways that do not interfere with the child's sense of competence and self-esteem.

Developmental Profiles and Growth Patterns

Growth and Physical Characteristics

■ Gains 4 to 5 pounds (1.8–2.3 kg) per year; weighs an average of 38 to 45 pounds (17.3–20.5 kg).

■ Grows an average of 2 to 2.5 inches (5.1–6.4 cm) per year; is approximately 42 to 46 inches (106.7–116.8 cm) tall.

Figure 6-10 May begin losing "baby" teeth.

■ Heart rate (pulse) is approximately 90 to 110 beats per minute.
■ Respiratory rate ranges from twenty to thirty, depending on activity and emotional status.
■ Body temperature is stabilized at 98° to 99.4°F.
■ Head size is approximately that of an adult's.
■ May begin to lose "baby" (deciduous) teeth; Figure 6-10.
■ Body is adult-like in proportion.
■ Requires approximately 1,800 calories daily.
■ Visual acuity is 20/20 using the Snellen E chart.
■ Visual tracking and **binocular vision** are well developed.

Motor Development

■ Walks backward, heel to toe.
■ Walks unassisted up and down stairs, alternating feet.
■ Learns to turn somersaults (should be taught the right way in order to avoid injury).
■ Touches toes without flexing knees.
■ Walks a balance beam.
■ Learns to skip using alternative feet.
■ Catches a ball thrown from 3 feet away.
■ Rides a tricycle or wheeled toy with speed and skillful steering; some children learn to ride bicycles, usually with training wheels.

binocular vision—both eyes working together, sending a single image to the brain.

5-Year-Olds

Figure 6-11 Cuts on the line, but not always perfectly.

■ Jumps or hops forward ten times in a row without falling.
■ Balances on either foot with good control for ten seconds.
■ Builds three-dimensional structures with small cubes by copying from a picture or model.
■ Reproduces many shapes and letters: square, triangle, *A, I, O, U, C, H, L, T.*
■ Demonstrates fair control of pencil or marker; may begin to color within the lines.
■ Cuts on the line with scissors (not perfectly); Figure 6-11.
■ Establishes hand dominance for the most part.

Perceptual-Cognitive Development

■ Forms rectangle from two triangular cuts.
■ Builds steps with set of small blocks.
■ Understands concept of *same* shape, *same* size.
■ Sorts objects on the basis of two dimensions, such as color and form.
■ Sorts a variety of objects so that all things in the group have a single common feature (classification skill: all are food items or boats or animals).

- Understands the concepts of smallest and shortest; places objects in order from shortest to tallest, smallest to largest.
- Identifies objects with specified serial position: first, second, last.
- Rote counts to 20 and above; many children count to 100.
- Recognizes numerals from 1 to 10.
- Understands the concepts of less than: "Which bowl has less water?"
- Understands the terms *dark, light,* and *early:* "I got up early, before anyone else. It was still dark."
- Relates clock time to daily schedule: "Time to turn on television when the little hand points to 5."
- Some children can tell time on the hour: five o'clock, two o'clock.
- Knows what a calendar is for.
- Recognizes and identifies penny, nickel, and dime; beginning to count and save money.
- Knows alphabet; many children can name upper- and lowercase letters.
- Understands the concept of half; can say how many pieces an object has when it's been cut in half.
- Asks innumerable questions: Why? What? Where? When?
- Eager to learn new things.

Speech and Language Development

- Has vocabulary of 1,500 words or more.
- Tells a familiar story while looking at pictures in a book.
- Uses functional definitions: a ball is to bounce; a bed is to sleep in.
- Identifies and names four to eight colors.
- Recognizes the humor in simple jokes; makes up jokes and riddles.
- Produces sentences with five to seven words; much longer sentences are not unusual.
- States the name of own city or town, birthday, and parents' names.
- Answers telephone appropriately; calls person to phone or takes a brief message.
- Produces speech that is almost entirely intelligible.
- Uses "would" and "could" appropriately.
- Uses past tense of irregular verbs consistently: "went," "caught," "swam."
- Uses past-tense inflection (-ed) appropriately to mark regular verbs: "jumped," "rained," "washed."

Personal-Social Development

- Enjoys friendships; often has one or two special playmates.
- Shares toys, takes turns, plays cooperatively (with occasional lapses); is often quite generous.

5-Year-Olds

Figure 6-12 Enjoys activities with other children.

- Participates in group play and shared activities with other children; suggests imaginative and elaborate play ideas; Figure 6-12.
- Is affectionate and caring, especially toward younger or injured children and animals.
- Follows directions and carries out assignments most of the time; generally does what parent or teacher requests.
- Continues to need adult comfort and reassurance, but may be less open in seeking and accepting comfort.
- Has better self-control; fewer dramatic swings of emotions.
- Likes to tell jokes, entertain, and make people laugh.
- Boasts about accomplishments.

5-Year-Olds

Daily Routines

Five-Year-Olds

Eating

- Eats well, but not at every meal.
- Likes familiar foods; prefers most vegetables raw.
- Often adopts food dislikes of family members and teachers.
- "Makes" breakfast (pours cereal, gets out milk and juice) and lunch (spreads peanut butter and jam on bread).

Toileting, Bathing, Dressing

- Takes full responsibility for own toileting; may put off going to the bathroom until an accident occurs or is barely avoided.
- Bathes fairly independently, but needs some help getting started.
- Dresses self completely; learning to tie shoes, sometimes aware when clothing is on wrong side out or backward.
- Careless with clothes; leaves them strewn about; needs many reminders to pick them up.
- Uses tissue for blowing nose, but often does a careless or incomplete job; forgets to throw tissue away.

Sleeping

- Manages all routines associated with getting ready for bed independently; can help with younger brother's or sister's bedtime routine.
- Averages ten or eleven hours of sleep per night. The five-year-old may still nap.
- Dreams and nightmares are common.
- Delays going to sleep if the day has been especially exciting or if long-anticipated events are scheduled for the next day.

Play and Social Activities

- Carries out family chores and routines; is usually helpful and cooperative.
- Knows the "right" way to do something and has the "right" answers to questions; somewhat opinionated and rigid in beliefs.
- Remains attached to home and family; willing to have an adventure, but wants the adventure to begin and end at home; fearful that mother may not come back.
- Plays well with other children, but three may be a crowd: two five-year-olds will often exclude the third.
- Shows affection and protection toward younger sister or brother; may feel over-burdened at times if younger child demands too much attention.

Learning Activities

Tips for parents and teachers:

■ Provide inexpensive materials (computer paper, wallpaper books, paint samples, scraps of fabric) for cutting, pasting, painting, coloring, folding; offer such things as simple looms for weaving, easy sewing activities, smaller beads for stringing; wood scraps and tools for simple carpentry.

■ Continue to collect props and dress-up clothes that allow more detailed acting out of family and worker roles; visit and talk about community activities—house building, post office and mail pickups, farmers' market; encourage play with puppets; assist in creating a stage (a cut-out carton works well).

■ Use a variety of books to help the child learn about the many joys and functions of books in everyday life; continue to read aloud, regularly and frequently.

■ Encourage the growing interest in paper-and-pencil games and number-, letter-, and word-recognition games that the child often invents, but may need adult help in carrying out.

■ Plan cooking experiences that allow the child to chop vegetables, roll out cookies, measure, mix, and stir.

■ Help set up improvised target games that promote eye–hand coordination: bean bag toss, bowling, ring toss, low hoop and basketball; ensure opportunities for vigorous play: wheel toys; jungle gyms and parallel bars; digging, raking, and hauling.

Developmental Alerts

Check with a health care provider or early childhood specialist if, by the sixth birthday, the child *does not*:

■ Alternate feet when walking up and down stairs.

■ Speak in a moderate voice; neither too loud, too soft, too high, too low.

■ Follow simple directions in stated order: "Please go to the cupboard, get a cup, and bring it to me."

■ Use four to five words in acceptable sentence structure.

■ Cut on a line with scissors.

- Sit still and listen to an entire short story (five to seven minutes).

- Maintain eye contact when spoken to (unless this is a cultural taboo).

- Play well with other children.

- Perform most self-grooming tasks independently: brush teeth, wash hands and face.

Safety Concerns

Continue to implement Safety Concerns described for the previous stages. Be aware of new safety issues as the child continues to grow and develop:

Falls

- Monitor parks and play areas for potential hazards, such as broken glass, defective equipment, sharp objects, deep holes, or inadequate cushioning material under play equipment.

Toys

- Refrain from purchasing toys that require electricity; battery-operated toys are safer.

Traffic

- Teach street safety, especially to children who walk to and from school; review safe practices often.

- Make sure that recommended car seats/restraints are appropriate for child's increasing weight/height.

Personal Safety

- *Never* leave children in a vehicle unattended for any length of time; temperatures (heat or cold) inside of a closed vehicle can quickly become deadly.

- Teach children a code word that can be used by persons authorized to pick them up from school.

Poisoning

- Only use nontoxic art supplies; check product labels carefully (http://www.cpsc.gov for product information).

5-Year-Olds

SUMMARY

Preschoolers, three-, four-, and five-year olds, are on the move every waking moment and eager to learn about everything. They need a great deal of support and approval from adults, although this need becomes less obvious as they move out of the preschool and into the primary years. Parents and teachers play a major role in providing guidance and the types of learning opportunities that enable preschoolers to practice, refine, and extend the vast number of skills that define healthy development. At the same time, adults must set limits that protect children from unforeseen consequences of their exuberance and determination to *grow up* that might be harmful to themselves or others. Each age-related section of the chapter closes with specific guidelines for adults as to what to expect from each age, how to support development in each area, and how to identify a possible developmental problem.

KEY TERMS

binocular vision	hand dominance
gender	tripod grasp

APPLY YOUR KNOWLEDGE

A. Apply What You Have Learned

Reread the developmental sketch about Anna and Juan at the beginning of the chapter. How might you answer the following questions?

1. Assuming that Juan's motor development is progressing typically, what skills would you expect to observe?

2. Would you consider Juan's personal-social development appropriate for his age?

3. What social behaviors would be typical for a four-year-old?

4. How would you respond to Anna's question if she asked, "How much responsibility can I expect Juan to assume for his own personal care at his age?"

5. In addition to reading bedtime stories, what other types of activities might Anna engage in with Juan to further his language development?

6. Is it developmentally appropriate to expect Juan to identify and name six colors, count to 100, understand simple fractions (e.g., 1/2, 1/4), and begin to tell time? Explain.

B. **Review Questions**

1. List three motor skills that appear between two and five years of age.

2. List a personal-social skill typical of each of the following ages: three-year-olds; four-year-olds; five-year olds.

3. List three major speech and language skills that appear between three and five years of age (in order).

 HELPFUL WEB SITES

Action Alliance for Children (diversity)	http://www.4children.org
Center for the Improvement of Early Reading Achievement	http://www.ciera.org
Child Trends	http://www.childtrends.org
Culturally & Linguistically Appropriate Services, Early Childhood Research Institute	http://ericps.crc.uiuc.edu/clas
Early Childhood Resource Center	http://www.rti.org/child
Parent Center	http://www.parentcenter.com
National Association for the Education of Young Children	http://www.naeyc.org

 **For additional child development resources, visit our Web site www.earlychilded.delmar.com**

Early Childhood: Six-, Seven-, and Eight-Year-Olds

 OBJECTIVES

After reading this chapter, you should be able to:

- Describe several sensory experiences that would be developmentally appropriate for six-, seven-, and eight-year-olds.
- Explain why behavior problems and emotional outbursts may reappear during this stage.
- Contrast the speech and language skills of six- and eight-year-olds.
- Explain and demonstrate Piaget's concept of conservation.
- Identify signs of reading readiness.
- Discuss the role of friendships.

MEET JUAN AND HIS FRIEND SERGIO

For weeks, Juan, has repeatedly asked his mother when school begins. Soon to turn seven, he is eagerly anticipating the start of first grade, riding on a school bus, and eating lunch in the cafeteria. Juan met his new teacher, Mr. Rosales, last week during the open house and is excited about having a "man teacher." His mother, Anna, thinks Juan will benefit from having a male role model, since his father has stopped their weekend visits.

Juan is also happy that his best friend, Sergio, will be in the same class. Unlike Juan, who is an only child, Sergio is the youngest of five brothers and three sisters. His parents work long hours and have little time or interest in helping Sergio advance academically. They view their role primarily as caretakers, and feel that the school is responsible for teaching their son. Sergio struggles to write his name, has difficulty sorting objects by category, and is unable to recognize and order numbers consistently. His kindergarten teacher was reluctant to advance him to the first grade, but Mr. Rosales assured her that he will devote extra time and attention to helping Sergio. Mr. Rosales is aware that Sergio's family speaks little English at home and has limited resources.

Juan thinks it is "pretty neat" that he will go to school all day like his mother, who plans to finish her associate's degree in early education this spring. She is proud of her son's progress in school and continues to work with him at home so that he will do well. Juan's advanced reading and writing skills are apparent in the imaginative stories he composes on the school's computer. When he is finished, Juan seeks out the teacher so he can read the story to him. Juan is also learning to tell time, and constantly wants his mother to ask him the time.

SIX-, SEVEN-, AND EIGHT-YEAR-OLDS

The period following the preschool years is especially remarkable. Children are in a stage of developmental integration, organizing and combining various developmental skills to accomplish increasingly complex tasks. At this age, boys and girls alike are becoming increasingly competent at taking care of their own personal needs—washing, dressing, toileting, eating, getting up, and getting ready for school. They observe family rules about mealtimes, television, and needs for privacy; Figure 7-1. They can be trusted to run errands and carry out simple responsibilities at home and school. In other words, these children are in control of themselves and their immediate world. Above all, six-, seven-, and eight-year-olds are ready and eager to go to school, even though somewhat apprehensive when the time actually arrives. Going to school creates anxieties, such as arriving on time, remembering to bring back assigned items, and walking home alone or to after-school child care.

Learning to read is the most complex perceptual task the child encounters following the preschool years. Recognizing visual letter symbols and associating them with their spoken sound is an important component of emerging literacy. It also means that children must learn to combine letters to form words, and to put these words together to form intelligible thoughts that can be read or spoken. Complex as the task is, most children between six and eight years of age become so adept at reading that the skill is soon taken for granted.

Sensory activities are essential to all learning in young children. Developmental kindergartens and primary classes recognize this. They emphasize sensory experiences by encouraging children to manipulate many kinds of materials—blocks; puzzles; paints, glue, paper, and found materials; sand, water and dirt;

Figure 7-1 Understands and respects family rules.

musical instruments and measurement devices. They also provide many opportunities for projects, such as cooking, gardening, carpentry, and dramatic play. The hands-on approach to the education of six-, seven-, and eight-year-olds, as well as younger children, is strongly endorsed by the National Association for the Education of Young Children (NAEYC). The philosophy is clearly presented in NAEYC's *Developmentally Appropriate Practices (DAP) in Early Childhood Programs Serving Children from Birth through Eight.*

Play continues to be one of the most important activities for fostering cognitive development in the early grades. It is also a major route to enhancing social development and all other developmental skills. For the most part, six-, seven-, and eight-year-olds play well with other children, especially if the group is not too large; Figure 7-2. There is keen interest in making friends, being a friend, and having friends. At the same time, there also may be quarreling, bossing, and excluding: "If you play with Lynette, then you're not *my* friend." Some children show considerable aggression, but it often tends to be verbal, aimed at hurting feelings rather than causing physical harm.

Friends are usually playmates that the child has ready access to in the neigh-

Figure 7-2 Children now tend to play well together.

borhood and at school. Friends often are defined as someone who is "fun," "pretty," "strong," or who "acts nice." Friendships at this age are easily established and readily abandoned; few are stable or long-lasting.

Throughout the primary school years, many children seem almost driven by the need to do everything right. On the other hand, they enjoy being challenged and completing tasks. They also like to make recognizable products and to join in organized activities. Most children enjoy these early school years. They become comfortable with themselves, their parents, and their teachers.

The Six-Year-Old

Exciting adventures begin to open up to six-year-olds as their coordination improves and their size and strength increase. New challenges often are met with a mixture of enthusiasm and frustration. Six-year-olds typically have difficulty making choices, and, at times, are overwhelmed by unfamiliar situations. At the same time, changes in their cognitive abilities enable them to see rules as useful for understanding everyday events and the behavior of others.

For many children, this period also marks the beginning of formal, subject-oriented schooling (it should be noted that formal academic activities at this age are considered developmentally inappropriate by many early childhood educators). Behavior problems or signs of tension, such as tics, nail-biting, or bed-wetting may flair up. Generally, these pass as children become familiar with new expectations and responsibilities associated with going to school. Despite the turmoil and trying times (for adults as well), most six-year-olds experience an abundance of good times marked by a lively curiosity, an eagerness to learn, an endearing sense of humor, and exuberant outbursts of affection and good will.

Developmental Profiles and Growth Patterns

Growth and Physical Characteristics

- Growth occurs slowly, but steadily.
- Height increases 2 to 3 inches (5–7.5 cm) each year: girls are an average of 42 to 46 inches (105–115 cm) tall, boys, 44 to 47 inches (110–117.5 cm).
- Weight increases 5 to 7 pounds (2.3–3.2 kg) a year: girls weigh approximately 38 to 47 pounds (19.1–22.3 kg), boys, 42 to 49 pounds (17.3–21.4 kg).
- Weight gains reflect significant increases in muscle mass.
- Heart rate (80 beats per minute) and respiratory rates (eighteen to twenty-eight breaths per minute) are similar to those of adults; rates vary with activity.
- Body takes on a lanky appearance as long bones of the arms and legs begin a phase of rapid growth.
- Loses "baby" (deciduous) teeth; permanent (secondary) teeth erupt, beginning with the two upper front teeth; girls tend to lose teeth at an earlier age than boys.
- Visual acuity should be 20/20; children testing 20/40 or less should have a professional evaluation.
- Farsightedness is not uncommon, often due to immature development (shape) of the eyeball.
- Develops more adult-like facial features.
- Requires approximately 1,600 to 1,700 calories per day.

deciduous teeth—initial set of teeth that eventually fall out; often referred to as "baby teeth."

6-Year-Olds

Figure 7-3 Shows improved ability to write numbers and letters.

Motor Development

■ Has increased muscle strength; typically, boys are stronger than girls of similar size.

■ Gains greater control over large and fine motor skills; movements are more precise and deliberate, although some clumsiness persists.

■ Enjoys vigorous physical activity: running, jumping, climbing, and throwing.

■ Moves constantly, even when trying to sit still.

■ Has increased dexterity and eye–hand coordination along with improved motor functioning, which facilitates learning to ride a bicycle, swim, swing a bat, or kick a ball.

■ Enjoys art projects: likes to paint, model with clay, "make things," draw and color, work with wood.

■ Writes numbers and letters with varying degrees of precision and interest; may reverse or confuse certain letters: *b/d, p/g, g/q, t/f;* Figure 7-3.

■ Traces around hand and other objects.

■ Folds and cuts paper into simple shapes.

■ Ties own shoes (still a struggle for some children).

Perceptual-Cognitive Development

■ Shows increased attention span; works at tasks for longer periods of time, although concentrated effort is not always consistent.

■ Understands concepts, such as simple time markers (today, tomorrow, yesterday) or uncomplicated concepts of motion (cars go faster than bicycles).

■ Recognizes seasons and major holidays and the activities associated with each.

■ Enjoys the challenge of puzzles, counting and sorting activities, paper-and-pencil mazes, and games that involve matching letters and words with pictures.

■ Recognizes some words by sight; attempts to sound out words (some children may be reading well by this time).

■ Identifies familiar coins: pennies, nickels, dimes, quarters.

■ Names and correctly holds up right and left hands fairly consistently.

■ Clings to certain beliefs involving magic or fantasy: the Tooth Fairy swapping a coin for a tooth; Santa Claus bringing gifts.

■ Arrives at some understanding about death and dying; often expresses fear that parents may die, especially mother.

Speech and Language Development

■ Loves to talk, often nonstop; may be described as a chatterbox.

■ Carries on adult-like conversations; asks many questions.

■ Learns as many as five to ten new words each day; vocabulary consists of 10,000 to 14,000 words.

■ Uses appropriate verb tenses, word order, and sentence structure.

■ Uses language rather than tantrums or physical aggression to express displeasure: "That's mine! Give it back, you dummy."

■ Talks self through steps required in simple problem-solving situations (although the "logic" may be unclear to adults).

■ Imitates slang and profanity; finds "bathroom" talk extremely funny.

■ Delights in telling jokes and riddles; often, the humor is far from subtle; Figure 7-4.

■ Enjoys being read to and making up stories.

■ Is capable of learning more than one language; does so spontaneously in a bi- or multilingual family.

Personal-Social Development

■ Experiences sudden mood swings: may be "best of friends" one minute, "worst of enemies" the next; loving one day, uncooperative and irritable the next; especially unpredictable toward mother or primary caregiver.

6-Year-Olds

Figure 7-4 Loves to talk silly and make up jokes.

- Becomes less dependent on parents as friendship circle expands; still needs closeness and nurturing, yet has urges to break away and "grow up."
- Needs and seeks adult approval, reassurance, and praise; anxious to please; may complain excessively about minor hurts to gain more attention.
- Continues to be self-centered (egocentric); still sees events almost entirely from own perspective: views everything and everyone as there for child's own benefit.
- Easily disappointed and frustrated by self-perceived failure.
- Has difficulty composing and soothing self; cannot tolerate being corrected or losing at games; may sulk, cry, refuse to play, or reinvent rules to suit own purposes.
- Is enthusiastic and inquisitive about surroundings and everyday events.
- Shows little or no understanding of ethical behavior or moral standards; often fibs, cheats, or "steals" objects belonging to others.
- Knows when he or she has been "bad"; values of "good" and "bad" are based on expectations and rules of parents and teachers.
- May be increasingly fearful of thunderstorms, the dark, unidentified noises, dogs and other animals.

6-Year-Olds

Daily Routines

Six-Year-Olds

Eating

■ Has a good appetite most of the time; often takes larger helpings than is able to finish. May skip an occasional meal; usually makes up for it later.

■ Has strong food preferences and definite dislikes; willingness to try new foods is unpredictable.

■ Uses table manners that often do not meet adult standards; may revert to eating with fingers; stuffs mouth; continues to spill milk or drop food in lap.

■ Has difficulty using table knife for cutting and fork for anything but spearing food.

■ Finds it difficult to sit through an entire meal; wiggles and squirms, gets off (or "falls" off) chair, drops utensils.

Toileting, Bathing, Dressing

■ Balks at having to take a bath; finds many excuses for delaying or avoiding a bath entirely.

■ Manages toileting routines without much help; sometimes is in a hurry or waits too long so that "accidents" happen.

■ Reverts to accidental soiling or wetting of pants during new experiences, such as the first weeks of school.

■ Sleeps through most nights without having to get up to use the bathroom. *Note:* Some children, especially boys, may not maintain a dry bed for another year or so.

■ Is careless about handwashing, bathing, and other self-care routines; needs frequent supervision and demonstrations to make sure they are carried out properly.

■ Expresses interest in selecting own clothes; needs guidance in determining occasions and seasonal appropriateness.

■ Drops clothing on floor or bed, loses shoes around the house, flings jacket down and often forgets where it is; Figure 7-5.

Sleeping

■ Needs nine to eleven hours of uninterrupted sleep.

■ Sleeps through the night; some children continue to have nightmares.

■ Sometimes requests a night-light, special blanket, or favorite stuffed toy (may want all three).

■ Finds numerous ways to avoid bedtime; when finally in bed, falls asleep quickly.

■ Finds ways to amuse self with books, toys, television, or coloring if awake before parents.

6-Year-Olds

Figure 7-5 Forgetful about caring for clothes.

Play and Social Activities

■ Has strong sense of self which is evident in terms of preferences and dislikes; uncompromising about wants and needs (often these do not coincide with adult plans or desires).

■ Is possessive about toys and books, parents and friends, but is able to share on some occasions.

■ Forms close, friendly relationship with one or two other children (often slightly older); play involves working together toward specific goals.

■ Becomes intolerant of being told what to do; may revert to tantrums.

■ Seeks teacher's attention, praise, reassurance; now views teacher (rather than parent) as the ultimate source of "truth."

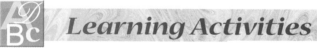 *Learning Activities*

Tips for parents and teachers:

■ Provide materials for coloring, cutting, pasting, painting.

■ Offer paper-and-pencil games: dot-to-dot, number-to-number, find-the-embedded items; copying and tracing activities.

■ Provide (and frequently join in) simple card games (Hearts, Old Maid) and board games, especially those where competitiveness is minimal.

■ Keep a plentiful supply of books on hand for the child to read and look at as well as for the adult to read to the child; encourage children to make up and tell stories.

■ Share children's interest in the collecting of objects; help them group, label, and display objects.

■ Provide an assortment of dress-up clothes for boys and girls; use children's interests and familiar community workers as a guide for role-play.

■ Encourage simple cooking, carpentry, and construction activities with blocks, cars, trucks, planes, zoo, and farm animals. (Avoid battery-driven and other mechanical toys—once the novelty has worn off they offer little involvement, hence little learning.)

■ Encourage bicycling, roller blading, swimming, experimenting on monkey bars, digging, throwing, catching, and batting activities.

Developmental Alerts

Check with a health care provider or early childhood specialist if, by the seventh birthday, the child *does not:*

■ Show signs of ongoing growth: increasing height and weight; continuing motor development, such as running, jumping, balancing.

■ Show some interest in reading and trying to reproduce letters, especially own name.

■ Follow simple, multiple-step directions: "Finish your book, put it on the shelf, and then get your coat on."

■ Follow through with instructions and complete simple tasks: putting dishes in the sink, picking up clothes, finishing a puzzle. *Note:* All children forget. Task incompletion is not a problem unless a child *repeatedly* leaves tasks unfinished.

■ Begin to develop alternatives to excessive use of inappropriate behaviors in order to get own way.

6-Year-Olds

7-Year-Olds

■ Develop a steady decrease in tension-type behaviors that may have developed with starting school: repeated grimacing or facial tics; eye twitching; grinding of teeth; regressive soiling or wetting; frequent stomachaches; refusing to go to school.

Safety Concerns

Continue to implement Safety Concerns described for the previous stages. Be aware of new safety issues as the child continues to grow and develop:

Burns

■ Keep matches and lighters in locked storage.

Falls

■ Make sure clothing fits properly; skirts and pants that are too long can cause child to trip or become entangled in play equipment. Remind children to keep shoes tied.

■ Require children to wear helmets and other appropriate protective gear whenever they ride bikes, skateboards, or scooters.

Tools/Equipment

■ Store machinery and sharp instruments in a safe place, out of children's reach.

■ Teach children proper use of scissors, knives, and kitchen equipment.

Traffic

■ Review safety rules to follow in and around motor vehicles, when crossing streets, or riding a bicycle.

■ Discuss appropriate behavior on buses if your child rides one to school.

■ Always insist on children wearing seatbelts when riding in motor vehicles.

Water

■ Enroll children in swimming lessons and teach them proper safety rules to follow around pools. Have proper rescue equipment accessible.

■ *Never leave children unattended near water.*

The Seven-Year-Old

Seven-year-olds are becoming more aware of themselves as individuals. They work hard at being responsible, being "good," and doing it "right." They tend to take themselves seriously—too seriously at times. When they fail to live up to their own self- imposed expectations, they may sulk or become frustrated or withdrawn. It's as if children at seven are trying to think things through, integrate what they already know with the flood of new experiences coming their way. Worrying about what may or may not come to pass is also typical; for example, anticipating yet dreading second grade can create anxiety. Maybe the work will be too hard; maybe the teacher won't be "nice"; maybe the other kids won't be friendly.

At the same time, children of this age have many positive traits. They are more reasonable and willing to share and cooperate. They are becoming better listeners and better at understanding and following through on what they hear. They are able to stay on-task for longer periods of time. They strive mightily to do everything perfectly (which only increases their worry load). Because of these complicated feelings, parents and teachers need to accept the mood swings. It seems the moods reflect the child's overwhelming efforts to cope with the conflicts inherent in being a seven-year-old.

Developmental Profiles and Growth Patterns

Growth and Physical Characteristics

- Weight increase tends to be relatively small; a gain of 6 pounds (2.7 kg) per year is typical. Seven-year-olds weigh approximately 50 to 55 pounds (22.7–25 kg).
- Height increases an average of 2.5 inches (6.25 cm) per year. Girls are approximately 44 to 44.5 inches (110–116.3 cm) tall, boys, 46 to 49.5 inches (115–124 cm).
- Muscle mass is fairly equal for boys and girls.
- Physical growth continues slowly and steadily; a few girls may overtake some boys in height.
- Posture is more erect; arms and legs continuing to lengthen, giving a longer, leaner look to many seven-year-olds.
- Energy level comes and goes, fluctuating between spurts of high energy and intervals of temporary fatigue.
- May still have a number of colds and other minor illnesses; however, these occur less frequently than at age six.
- Eyeballs continue to change shape and size; vision should be checked periodically to ensure good sight.
- Hair often grows darker in color.
- Baby teeth continue to be replaced by permanent teeth.

Figure 7-6 Shows continued improvement of large motor skills.

Motor Development

■ Exhibits large and fine motor control that is more finely tuned: balances on either foot, runs up and down stairs with alternating feet, throws and catches smaller balls, practices batting balls, manipulates a computer mouse with greater precision; Figure 7-6.

■ Tends to be cautious in undertaking more challenging physical activities, such as climbing up or jumping down from high places.

■ Practices a new motor skill over and over until mastered, then drops it to work on something else.

■ Finds floor more comfortable than furniture when reading or watching television; legs often in constant motion.

■ Uses knife and fork appropriately, but inconsistently.

■ Holds pencil in a tight grasp near the tip; rests head on forearm, lowers head almost to the table top when doing pencil-and-paper tasks.

■ Produces letters and numbers in a deliberate and confident fashion: characters are increasingly uniform in size and shape; may run out of room on line or page when writing.

Perceptual-Cognitive Development

■ Understands concepts of space and time in ways that are both logical and more practical: a year is "a long time"; 100 miles is "far away."
■ Begins to grasp Piaget's concepts of conservation: for example, the shape of a container does not necessarily reflect the quantity it can hold.
■ Gains a better understanding of cause and effect: "If I'm late for school again, I'll be in big trouble."
■ Tells time by the clock and also understands calendar time—days, months, years, and seasons.
■ Plans ahead: "I'm saving this cookie for tonight."
■ Shows marked fascination with magic tricks; enjoys putting on "shows" for parents and friends.
■ Finds reading easier; many seven-year-olds read for their own enjoyment and delight in retelling story details.
■ Tends to have better reading than spelling skills.
■ Enjoys counting and saving money; Figure 7-7.
■ Continues to reverse letters and substitute sounds on occasion.

Speech and Language Development

■ Enjoys storytelling; likes to write short stories, tell imaginative tales.
■ Uses adult-like sentence structure and language in conversation; patterns reflect cultural and geographical differences.
■ Becomes more precise and elaborate in use of language; greater use of descriptive adjectives and adverbs.
■ Uses gestures to illustrate conversations.
■ Criticizes own performance: "I didn't draw that right," "Her picture is better than mine."
■ Verbal exaggeration commonplace: "I ate ten hot dogs at the picnic."
■ Offers explanations of events in terms of own preferences or needs: "It didn't rain because I was going on a picnic."
■ Describes personal experiences in great detail: "First we parked the car, then we hiked up this long trail, then we sat down on a broken tree near a lake and ate . . ."
■ Understands and carries out multiple-step instructions (up to five steps); may need to have directions repeated because of not listening to entire request the first time.
■ Enjoys writing e-mail messages and simple notes to friends.

conservation—the stage in children's cognitive development when they understand that an object's physical qualities (e.g., weight, mass) remain the same despite changes in its appearance; for example, flattening a ball of playdough does not affect its weight.

Figure 7-7 Interested in counting and saving money.

Personal-Social Development

■ Is cooperative and affectionate toward adults and less frequently annoyed with them; sees humor in everyday happenings and is more outgoing.

■ Likes to be the "teacher's helper"; eager for teacher's attention and approval, but less obvious about seeking it.

■ Seeks out friendships; friends are important, but can find plenty to do if no one is available.

■ Quarrels less often, although squabbles and tattling continue to occur in both one-on-one and group play.

■ Complains that family decisions are unjust; that a particular sibling gets to do more or is given more.

■ Blames others for own mistakes; makes up alibis for personal shortcomings: "I could have made a better one, but my teacher didn't give me enough time."

■ Prefers same-gender playmates; more likely to play in groups.

■ Worries about not being liked; feelings easily hurt; may cry, be embarrassed, or state adamantly, "I will never play with you again" when criticized.

■ Takes responsibilities seriously; can be trusted to carry out directions and commitments; worries about being late for school or not getting work done.

Daily Routines

Seven-Year-Olds

Eating

■ Eats most foods; better about sampling unfamiliar foods or taking small tastes of disliked foods, but still refuses a few strong "hates."

■ Shows interest in food; likes to help with grocery shopping and meal preparation.

■ Uses table manners that are far from perfect, but improving; less spilled milk and other "accidents" due to silliness or haste to finish.

■ Uses eating utensils with relative ease; seldom eats with fingers; some children still have trouble cutting meat.

■ Dawdles less over meals, although easily distracted by things going on elsewhere in the house or outdoors.

Toileting, Bathing, Dressing

■ Dawdles at bathtime; however, once in the tub, seems to enjoy the experience; can manage own bath with a minimum of help.

■ Dresses self; dawdling continues, but child can speed up when time becomes critical.

■ Buttons and zips own clothes; ties own shoes; often careless: buttons askew, shoelaces soon dragging; Figure 7-8.

■ Shows little interest in clothes; wears whatever is laid out or available.

■ Shows more interest in combing or brushing own hair.

■ Has good bowel and bladder control; individual rhythm well established; may resist having bowel movements at school.

■ Less likely to get up during the night to use the toilet.

Sleeping

■ Averages ten to eleven hours of sleep at night; children who are in bed fewer hours, often have trouble getting up in the morning.

■ Sleeps soundly with few if any bad dreams; instead, often dreams about own exploits and adventures.

■ Gets ready for bed independently most nights, but still enjoys being tucked in or read to.

■ Wakes up early most mornings; occupies self in bed with toys, counting out savings in piggy bank, looking at baseball card collection, reading.

Figure 7-8 Often needs reminding about tying shoes.

Play and Social Activities

■ Enjoys participating in organized group activities (Boys' and Girls' Clubs, Cub Scouts and Brownies, swim and soccer teams).

■ Dislikes missing school or social events; wants to "keep up" with friends and classmates.

■ Has interest in coloring and cutting things out, with a friend or alone.

■ Engages in favorite play activities, such as bicycle riding, climbing activities, skating, and computer games.

■ Likes to play competitive board and card games, but may bend the rules when losing.

Learning Activities

Tips for parents and teachers:

■ Make trips to the library for children's story time and dramatic play activities as well as books.

■ Sign up for free or low-cost community offerings of interest to the child: art, science, swimming, dancing, museum programs.

■ Take family "collecting walks" in the neighborhood, on nearby beaches, or in parks; support child's efforts to organize "treasures."

■ Accumulate tools and equipment that really work: simple carpentry and garden tools, science materials (growing a potato vine, maintaining an ant farm or a simple aquarium).

- Gather materials for creating art projects, models, science experiments: pieces of wood, plastic, various weights and textures of cardboard and paper, beads, fabric, yarn.

- Offer dress-up clothes and props for planning and staging "shows"; attend the performances.

- Provide doll house, farm or zoo set, service station or airport, complete with small-scale people, animals, and equipment.

Developmental Alerts

Check with a health care provider or early childhood specialist if, by the eighth birthday, the child *does not*:

- Attend to the task at hand; show longer periods of sitting quietly, listening, responding appropriately.

- Follow through on simple instructions.

- Go to school willingly most days (of concern are excessive complaints about stomachaches or headaches when getting ready for school).

- Make friends (observe closely to see if the child plays alone most of the time or withdraws consistently from contact with other children).

- Sleep soundly most nights (frequent and recurring nightmares or bad dreams are usually at a minimum at this age).

- Seem to see or hear adequately at times (squints, rubs eyes excessively, asks frequently to have things repeated).

- Handle stressful situations without undue emotional upset (excessive crying, sleeping or eating disturbances, withdrawal, frequent anxiety).

- Assume responsibility for personal care (dressing, bathing, feeding self) most of the time.

- Show improved motor skills.

Safety Concerns

Continue to implement Safety Concerns described for the previous stages. Be aware of new safety issues as the child continues to grow and develop:

Firearms

■ Store unloaded guns in a locked cabinet. Teach children to stay away from guns and to immediately report any that are found. Check with parents of your children's friends to determine if guns are present and properly stored in their house.

Play Environments

■ Review rules for safe use of playground equipment and safe play when away from home. Be aware of your child's friends and types of play they tend to engage in.

Tools/Equipment

■ Do not let children use power mowers or other yard equipment (e.g., weed eaters, hedge trimmers) ; keep children away when such equipment is in use.

Water

■ Continue to monitor children at all times when they are in a pool, lake, or other body of water.

The Eight-Year-Old

Eight-year-olds display a great enthusiasm for life. Energy is concentrated on improving skills they already possess and enhancing what they already know. Eight-year-olds once again experience strong feelings of independence and are eager to make decisions about their own plans and friends. Interests and attention are increasingly devoted to peers and team or group activities rather than parents, teachers, or siblings. Sometime near midyear, boys and girls go their separate ways and form new interests in same-gender groups.

Developmental Profiles and Growth Patterns

Growth and Physical Characteristics

■ Continues to gain 5 to 7 pounds (2.3–3.2 kg) per year; an eight-year-old weighs approximately 55 to 61 pounds (25–27.7 kg). Girls typically weigh less than boys.

■ Height increases at a pace that is slow, but steady. Grows an average of 2.5 inches (6.25 cm) per year; girls are often taller (46 to 49 inches [115–122.5 cm]) as compared to boys (48 to 52 inches [120–130 cm]).

■ Body shape takes on a more mature appearance; arms and legs grow longer, creating an image that is tall and lanky.

■ Normal vision acuity is 20/20. Vision should be checked periodically to ensure good sight.

■ Some girls may begin to develop breasts and pubic hair, and experience menses.

■ Mood swings may become more apparent as changes in hormonal activity occur.

■ Overall state of health improves; experiences fewer illnesses.

Motor Development

■ Enjoys vigorous activity; likes to dance, roller blade, swim, wrestle, ride bikes, and fly kites.

■ Seeks out opportunities to participate in team activities and games, such as soccer, baseball, and kickball.

■ Exhibits significant improvement in agility, balance, speed, and strength.

■ Copies words and numbers from blackboard with increasing speed and accuracy; has good eye–hand coordination.

■ Possesses seemingly endless energy.

Perceptual-Cognitive Development

■ Collects objects; organizes and displays items according to more complex systems; bargains and trades with friends to obtain additional pieces.

■ Saves money for small purchases; eagerly develops plans to earn cash for odd jobs; studies catalogues and magazines for ideas of items to purchase.

■ Begins taking an interest in what others think and do; understands there are differences of opinion, cultures, distant countries.

■ Accepts challenge and responsibility with enthusiasm; delights in being asked to perform tasks, both at home and in school; interested in being rewarded for efforts; Figure 7-9.

■ Likes to read and work independently; spends considerable time planning and making lists.

■ Understands perspective (shadow, distance, shape); drawings reflect more realistic portrayal of objects.

■ Begins to understand elementary principles of conservation: while jars that are tall and narrow may look different from those that are short and wide, they may hold the same amount.

■ Uses more sophisticated logic in efforts to understand everyday events; for example, is systematic in looking for a misplaced jacket or toy.

Figure 7-9 Enjoys challenge and participation in group activities.

■ Adds and subtracts multiple-digit numbers; learning multiplication and division.
■ Looks forward to school and is disappointed when ill or unable to attend.

Speech and Language Development

■ Delights in telling jokes and riddles.
■ Understands and carries out multiple-step instructions (up to five steps); may need to have directions repeated because of not listening to the entire request.
■ Enjoys writing letters or sending e-mail messages to friends; includes descriptions that are imaginative and detailed; Figure 7-10.
■ Uses language to criticize and compliment others; repeats slang and curse words.
■ Understands and follows rules of grammar in conversation and written form.
■ Is intrigued with learning secret word codes and using code language.
■ Converses fluently with adults; able to think and talk about past and future: "What time are we leaving to get to the swim meet next week?"

Figure 7-10 Writes letters with imaginative detail.

Personal-Social Development

■ Begins forming opinions about moral values and attitudes; declares things either right or wrong.

■ Plays with two or three "best" friends, most often of the same age and gender; also enjoys spending some time alone.

■ Seems less critical of own performance, but is easily frustrated and upset when unable to complete a task or when the product does not meet expectations.

■ Enjoys team games and activities; group membership and acceptance by peers are important.

■ Continues to blame others or makes up alibis to explain own shortcomings or mistakes.

■ Enjoys talking on the telephone with friends.

■ Understands and respects the fact that some children are more talented in certain areas, such as drawing, sports, reading, art, or music.

■ Desires attention and recognition from teacher or parents; enjoys performing for adults and challenging them in games.

Eight-Year-Olds

Eating

- Has fairly hearty appetite; boys typically eat more than girls.
- Enjoys eating; willing to try new foods and some of the foods previously refused.
- Takes pride in using good table manners, especially when eating out or when company is present; at home, manners of less concern.
- Prefers to finish meal quickly in order to resume previous activities; may stuff mouth with too much food or not chew food thoroughly.

Toileting, Bathing, Dressing

- Develops a pattern for bowel and bladder functions; usually has good control, but may need to urinate more frequently when under stress.
- Hurries through handwashing; dirt tends to end up on towel rather than down the drain.
- Enjoys bath and playing in water; easily sidetracked when supposed to be getting ready to bathe; some children are able to prepare their own bath.
- Takes greater interest in appearance, selecting and coordinating own outfits, brushing hair, and looking good.
- Helps care for own clothes; hangs clothes up most times, helps with laundry by folding and returning items to dresser.
- Ties own shoes skillfully, but often too busy to be bothered.

Sleeping

- Sleeps soundly through the night (averages ten hours); efforts to delay bedtime may suggest less sleep is needed.
- Begins to question established bedtime; wants to stay up later; dawdles, becomes distracted while getting ready for bed.
- Sometimes wakes early and gets dressed while family members are still sleeping.

Play and Social Activities

- Enjoys competitive activities and sports (soccer, baseball, swimming, gymnastics); eager to join a team; just as eager to quit if too much forced competition.
- Begins to adopt a know-it-all attitude toward the end of the eighth year; becomes argumentative with peers (and adults).
- Likes to play board, electronic, and card games; often interprets rules so as to improve own chances of winning.
- Seeks acceptance from peers; begins to imitate clothing fads, hairstyles, behavior, and language of admired peers.

Learning Activities

Tips for parents and teachers:

■ Provide (and join in) games that require a moderate degree of strategy: checkers, dominoes, card games, magic sets, computer games.

■ Encourage creativity; provide materials for simple painting, crafts, cooking, or building projects.

■ Make frequent trips to the library; provide books to read, as well as stories on audio- and videocassettes.

■ Invest in an inexpensive camera; encourage children to experiment.

■ Arrange for opportunities to develop skills in noncompetitive activities—swimming, dancing, tumbling, skating, skiing, musical instruments; this is a time of *trying out* many interests; seldom is there a long-term commitment.

■ Assign routine tasks, such as feeding the dog, folding laundry, dusting furniture, bringing in the mail, or setting the dinner table to foster a sense of responsibility.

Developmental Alerts

Check with a health care provider or early childhood specialist if, by the ninth birthday, the child *does not*:

■ Exhibit a good appetite and continued weight gain (some children, especially girls, may already begin to show early signs of an eating disorder).

■ Experience fewer illnesses.

■ Show improved motor skills, in terms of agility, speed, and balance.

■ Understand abstract concepts and use complex thought processes to problem-solve.

■ Enjoy school and the challenge of learning.

■ Follow through on multiple-step instructions.

■ Express ideas clearly and fluently.

■ Form friendships with other children and enjoy participating in group activities.

8-Year-Olds

Safety Concerns

Continue to implement Safety Concerns described for the previous stages. Be aware of new safety issues as the child continues to grow and develop:

Animals

■ Remind children to avoid approaching unfamiliar animals and to refrain from yelling or making sudden movements.

■ Teach children to recognize poisonous snakes and to leave them alone.

■ Insist on good handwashing after touching any animal.

Backpacks

■ To prevent injury, backpacks should be worn over both shoulders, secured with a hip strap, loaded with the heaviest items against the back, and weigh less than 20 percent of the child's body weight. Wheeled backpacks are preferable.

Toys

■ Supervise use of more advanced toys, such as chemistry or woodworking sets, and those that involve electricity or propellants.

Water

■ Require children to wear a life jacket whenever boating, skiing, or participating in other water sports.

SUMMARY

The transition to formal schooling marks a distinctive change for many children. New experiences and opportunities are generally met with a combination of enthusiasm and improving abilities, as well as periodic reluctance and frustration. Children often set high expectations for themselves, then falter when these standards cannot be met. However, they are eager to learn and accomplish many complex skills, including reading, writing, telling time, counting money, and following detailed instructions during this stage. They become imaginative storytellers, jokesters, and even "magicians." Friends and friendships are increasingly important, as children's interests and independence expand. They also begin to understand the meaning and complexity of everyday events, form moral values and opinions, and recognize cultural and individual differences. By the end of this period, children are fully capable of managing their personal needs and grooming, but may still need occasional adult prompting.

 ## KEY TERMS

conservation	developmental integration
deciduous teeth	

APPLY YOUR KNOWLEDGE

A. Apply What You Have Learned

Reread the developmental sketch about Juan and Sergio at the beginning of the chapter. How might you answer the following questions?

1. What initial forms of screening would you arrange for Sergio to ensure that his learning delays weren't being caused by a health-related condition?

2. What types of motor skills would you expect Juan to exhibit if his development was typical for a seven-year-old?

3. From a developmental perspective, is it appropriate for Juan's mother to encourage his participation in a local youth soccer league?

4. How might differences in environmental conditions help to explain why Juan and Sergio are performing at different levels in school?

5. From a developmental perspective, explain Juan's persistent desire to demonstrate his newly acquired ability to tell time or read his stories to the teacher.

6. If you were Juan's mother, what special safety precautions should you be taking to prevent unintentional injury?

B. Review Questions

1. List one characteristic that describes the typical cognitive skill of a six-year-old, a seven-year-old, and an eight-year-old.

2. List three perceptual skills that indicate readiness to begin reading.

3. List three reasonable expectations for a six-year-old in terms of home routines.

4. List three developmentally appropriate activities that a parent or teacher might utilize to expand the language skills of seven- and eight-year-olds.

HELPFUL WEB SITES

Canadian Pediatric Society	http://www.cpa.ca
Center for Research on Education, Diversity & Excellence (CREDE)	http://www.cal.org/crede
Parent Soup	http://www.parentsoup.com
Safe Kids	http://www.safekids.org
Your Child's Health	http://www.yourchildshealth.echn.ca

For additional child development resources, visit our Web site www.earlychilded.delmar.com

Middle Childhood: Nine-, Ten-, Eleven-, and Twelve-Year-Olds

Chapter

8

OBJECTIVES

After reading this chapter, you should be able to:

- Describe several changes that occur during early puberty.
- Discuss how the ability to think abstractly affects learning.
- Describe the concept of friendship from the perspective of a nine- and a ten-year-old.
- Plan developmentally appropriate activities for nine- and ten-year-olds; eleven- and twelve-year-olds.
- Compare and contrast the language development of nine- to ten- and eleven- to twelve-year-olds.

MEET JUAN AND HIS STEPSISTER, CARLIN

Juan, age eleven, and his new stepfather have enjoyed each other's companionship from the very beginning. They spend considerable time together, attending sporting events, taking camping trips in the mountains, and building model planes. Juan likes school, especially math and computer classes, and has many "best friends." His teacher considers Juan a good student, and appreciates his offers to help around the classroom. Juan's parents are continually amazed by his seemingly endless appetite and energy.

Juan has slowly been adjusting to the idea of having a stepsister. Carlin, a caring and talkative nine-year-old, is somewhat less enthusiastic than Juan about school. During the last parent–teacher conference, Carlin's teachers expressed concern about her inability to remain seated and focused on assignments for longer than five or ten minutes at a time. Her mother has made similar observations at home, often becoming exasperated because Carlin seems unable to follow multistep directions and tends to be disorganized. It isn't uncommon for Carlin to "forget" when a book report is due, that the dog needs to be fed, or that she was supposed to bring home her list of spelling words for tomorrow's test. Carlin has few friends and prefers to play with Juan and his friends. However, Juan finds it annoying when she tags along, and frequently begs his father to make her stop.

NINE-, TEN-, ELEVEN-, AND TWELVE- YEAR OLDS

The stretch of years from age eight to early adolescence is usually an enjoyable and peaceful time for all concerned. Spontaneous behaviors are gradually channeled into more goal-directed efforts as children begin making the transition from a state of dependence to one of greater independence. While they are no longer young children, they are also not yet capable adults. This tension contributes to struggles with self-concept, self-esteem, and desire for complete autonomy.

The middle years are marked by a hunger for knowledge and understanding. Most children have adjusted to being at school for six or more hours each day. The stresses, strains, and frustrations of learning to read, write, do basic arithmetic, and follow directions are long forgotten. Language usage becomes more sophisticated and adult-like. During this period, children also develop an increasingly complex ability to think in the abstract, understand cause and effect, and use **logic** for solving problems and figuring out how things work. They comprehend that things really are the same in spite of being used for alternative purposes or seen from a different perspective—a shovel can not only be used for digging, but can also be handy for prying the lid off a paint can; a mixing bowl can be traced to draw a perfect circle.

Changes in physical growth and development vary greatly from child to child during this period; Figure 8-1. Girls in particular grow rapidly. Research finds that girls as young as eight or nine may already be experiencing hormonal changes associated with puberty. Some older children may begin to experiment with new behaviors, such as wearing alternative clothing and hair styles, quitting a sport or music lessons, forming associations with a "different crowd," smoking, or consuming alcohol. While parents may find this phase quite distressing, it is an important process that helps children determine what will ultimately be right for them.

---

logic—*process of reasoning based on a series of facts or events.*

Figure 8-1 Children's rate of growth and development often vary.

Nine- and Ten-Year-Olds

Most nine- and ten-year-olds have entered a phase of relative contentment—sometimes described as the calm before the storm of adolescence. While nine-year-olds may still display some emotional highs and lows, these outbursts gradually mellow by age ten. Home and family continue to serve as sources of security and comfort. Hugs and kisses are still offered as signs of affection for parents.

Most nine- and ten-year-olds also find school enjoyable. They eagerly anticipate classes and meeting with friends, and are dismayed when they are late or forced to miss a day. Teachers are respected and their attention is highly coveted. Small homemade gifts and offers of assistance are made in hopes of pleasing one's teacher. Despite a longer attention span, most children still need adequate opportunity to move about the classroom and participate in vigorous outdoor activity.

Developmental Profiles and Growth Patterns

Growth and Physical Characteristics

■ Rate of growth is slow and irregular; girls begin to experience growth spurts far more dramatically than do boys; boys are more alike in size.

■ Assumes a slimmer shape as fat accumulations begin to shift.

■ Growth of various body parts occurs at different rates; lower half of body grows faster; arms and legs appear long and out of proportion.

■ Brain increases significantly in size; almost reaches adult size by age ten.

■ Height increases approximately 2 inches (5 cm) each year; increases may be greater during growth spurts.

■ Gains approximately 6 1/2 pounds (14.3 kg) per year.

■ Loses remaining baby teeth; overcrowding may occur when larger, permanent teeth erupt into a yet small jaw.

■ Girls may begin to experience prepubertal changes (e.g., budding breasts, appearance of pubic hair, rounding of hips, accentuated waistline; darkening of hair color); boys are less likely to undergo any sexual changes for another year or two.

Motor Development

■ Throws a ball with accuracy; writes, sketches, and performs other fine motor skills with improved coordination. This period is marked by continued refinement of fine motor skills, especially notable among girls.

■ Uses arms, legs, hands, and feet with ease and improved precision; boys tend to excel in large motor activities.

■ Runs, climbs, skips rope, swims, rides bikes, and skates with skill and confidence; Figure 8-2.

■ Enjoys team sports, but may still need to develop some of the necessary complex skills.

■ Likes to use hands for arts and crafts, cooking, woodworking, needlework, and building or taking apart objects, such as a clock or telephone.

■ Draws pictures in detail; takes great joy in perfecting handwriting skills.

Perceptual-Cognitive Development

■ Develops ability to reason based more on logic than **intuition** (Piaget's stage of **concrete operational thought**); still sees some situations as either black or white, with "yes" or "no" answers, but begins thinking in less concrete, more creative ways.

■ Likes challenges in arithmetic, but doesn't always understand mathematical relationships involved in complex operations, such as multiplication or division.

---

intuition—thoughts and ideas based on a feeling or hunch.
concrete operational thought—Piaget's third stage of cognitive development; period when concepts of conservation and classification are understood.

Figure 8-2 Performs many activities now with skill and confidence.

- Learns best through hands-on learning; teachers' lectures are less effective than engagement in activities that produce the same information.
- Enjoys time at school; finds it difficult to sit still for periods longer than thirty minutes; forgets all about school as soon as it is over.
- Likes to use reading and writing skills for nonacademic activities: compiling grocery lists, composing scripts for puppet shows, drawing and labeling neighborhood maps.
- Shows improved understanding of cause and effect.
- Continues to master concepts of time, weight, volume, distance.
- Traces events based on recall; able to think in reverse, following a series of occurrences back to their beginning.

Speech and Language Development

- Loves to talk, often nonstop and for no specific reason; sometimes used as an attention-getting device.

Figure 8-3 Delights in telling jokes and riddles.

■ Expresses feelings and emotions effectively through words.

■ Understands language as a system for communicating with others.

■ Uses slang expressions commonly expressed by peers in conversation: "kinda," "right on," "awesome."

■ Recognizes that some words have double meanings, "sharp shoes," "cool haircut."

■ Finds humor in using illogical metaphors (play on words) in jokes and riddles; Figure 8-3.

■ Shows advanced understanding of grammatical sequences; recognizes when a sentence is not grammatically correct.

Personal-Social Development

■ Enjoys being with friends; seeks out friendships based on common interests and proximity (neighborhood children or classmates); is verbally critical of the opposite gender: "Boys are too rough," "Girls are babies."

■ Has several "good" friends and an "enemy" or two who may change from day to day.

■ Begins to show more interest in rules and basing games on realistic play; rules should be kept simple so everyone enjoys the game.

■ Responds with name-calling and teasing when provoked; less likely to use physical aggression than previously; also understands that such behavior can affect others' feelings.

Observing Children

What we know about children, how they grow, how they learn, how they interact with others, stems from first-hand observation. Early psychologists and educators such as Froebel, Pestalozzi, Freud, Montessori, Gesell, Skinner, and Piaget observed the daily activities of hundreds of infants and children. They recorded what they saw and heard as the children learned to walk and talk, identify shapes and colors, recognize numbers and letters, get along with others, reason, and solve problems.

These recorded observations provide the foundation for what we now know about child development, effective teaching, curriculum models, and the significance of the parent-child relationship.

TEACHERS AS CLASSROOM OBSERVERS

The benchmark of a quality early childhood program is regularly scheduled observations and frequent notetaking by the adults. Watching and recording what children actually do in the classroom and in the outdoor play area enables staff to design appropriate indoor and outdoor learning environments.

Teachers' observations are critical. They are trained in child development. They know what to expect of children. They can apply their knowledge effectively in an environment where children are "being themselves" and plan for the individual needs and differences among children.

At parent conferences, teachers rely on their observation records to cite concrete examples related to the child's progress. Written observations attest to the teacher's interest in each child and to the teacher's ability to communicate that interest to parents.

PARENTS AS CLASSROOM OBSERVERS

Parents must always be welcome in their child's classroom, whether as scheduled observers or on a drop-in basis. They have a right to see and question everything that occurs in the classroom and outside play area. When parents come for a scheduled observation, they can be given a clipboard and paper so they can make notes about whatever interests them; for example, what and whom their child plays with, or what seems to please or bother their child. In a follow-up discussion, teachers can learn how parents view the program and can explore mutual concerns and pleasure about the child's progress.

Parents' observations, made at home or at school, are invaluable. Parents know their child better than anyone else. They see their child under every imaginable circumstance. They are aware of the child's likes and dislikes, joys and anxieties. Most importantly, they know what they want for their child.

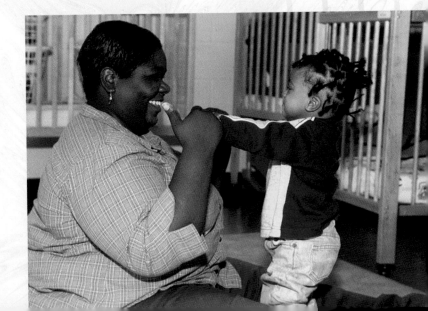

TYPES OF OBSERVATIONS

Recorded observations take many forms: anecdotal notes, running records and logs, samples of children's speech and language, frequency count and duration measures. Checklists and rating scales also rely on direct observations. A brief sampling of observation methods is given here. The annotated bibliography (Appendix 8) provides references for additional information.

Anecdotal Notes

Anecdotal notes are made on a small note pad (3 X 5 inches) carried in a pocket. The notes are brief, dated phrases about discrete behaviors observed in a given child. The notes can be used to track development in specific domains or to gather information about a specific concern.

Teachers take a minute or less several times a day to write down a few relevant words about what they see happening. Over time, the dated notes yield a composite picture. It may point to a need for special guidance plans. If so, continuing the notetaking enables teachers to see if the plan is helping the child. If there are no particular concerns, anecdotal notes, filed chronologically by developmental domains, are essential to placing a child, writing progress reports, and preparing for parent conferences.

Language Samples

To obtain a language sample, an observer writes down every utterance a child makes, exactly as the child says it. One purpose of the samplings, usually done over a month or so for 15 or 20 minutes at a time, is to track the child's speech and language development. Another purpose is to see if the child's language "works." Is the child communicating effectively? Does the child get what he or she needs and wants by using language? No other behaviors (except communicative gestures or facial grimaces) are recorded, though brief notations might be made; for example, that children rarely respond to the child's verbal overtures. Language samples are invaluable in planning individualized programs. They also are essential in preparing for parent conferences, which can be enlivened when teachers read amusing quips or insightful statements made by the child.

Frequency and Duration Counts

When concerns arise about a specific aspect of a child's behavior, teachers must first determine how often the behavior occurs (frequency) or how long it goes on (duration). Such counts are easily made while teachers carry out their other responsibilities. One type of frequency count simply requires the

teacher to make a tally mark every time the child engages in the specified behavior. A count may reveal, for example, that a two-year-old who was said to cry or hit "all the time" was actually doing so only once or twice a morning, some mornings not at all. For behaviors that occur at a high rate, teachers sometimes carry a golf stroke or knitting stitch counter.

A duration count (or measure) often consists of simply jotting down the time a child enters and leaves an area or activity. Another example would be penciling (unobtrusively) on a corner of a painting or collage the time the

child started and finished the project. These are but two examples of easy-to-make observations. A frequency count provides significant information as to whether a "problem" is really a problem. A duration count helps teachers decide if they need to try to enhance the child's span of attention in certain program areas.

Checklists

Checklists allow a teacher or other observer to quickly record the occurrence of a specified behavior or developmental achievement. In infant centers, many "firsts" can be checked off: the day Josie first smiled, rolled over, walked alone. In preschools, a checklist with children's names down one side and curriculum objectives across the top is useful. By inserting the date, teachers "check off" when Carmen correctly identified and

matched the primary colors; John J. built a tower of eight one-inch cubes; Arden zipped her jacket by herself. Checklists often are constructed by teachers to reflect program objectives. The lists, whether teacher-made or commercial, can be simple or detailed, depending on need (examples: Appendix 3).

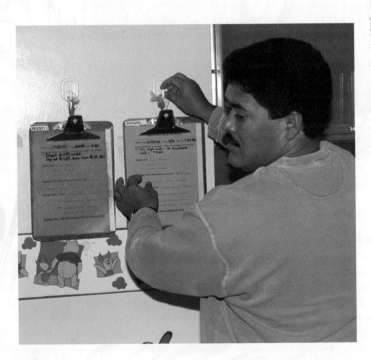

OBJECTIVITY WHEN OBSERVING

Objectivity means writing down only what the child actually does and says. It means that any two observers (two teachers, a teacher and a parent, a volunteer and an aide), observing the same child at the same time, produce identical reports of what the child actually did.

Reality-based information is essential for several reasons:

- It provides facts (not personal bias) in determining the extent to which a problem affects the child's developmental progress or the well-being of other children.

- It provides consensus and a firm base for arranging individualized learning activities.

- It is essential in tracking a child's progress in all developmental areas.

- It provides concrete information for conducting effective parent-teacher conferences

Figure 8-4 Admires teachers and adult club leaders.

■ Begins to develop moral reasoning; adopts social customs and moral values of one's society: honesty, right from wrong, fairness, good and bad, respect.

■ Develops attachments to teachers, coaches, club leaders; may see them as "heroes"; often goes out of way to please and gain their attention; Figure 8-4.

■ Acts with considerable confidence; knows everything and can do no wrong.

■ Takes criticism as a personal attack; feelings are easily hurt; has difficulty dealing with failure and frustration.

9- & 10-Year-Olds

Daily Routines

Nine- and Ten-Year-Olds

Eating

■ Appetite may fluctuate depending on vigor of activity; eats more with increased activity; prefers to eat when hungry rather than at prescribed times.

■ Eats any time of day, yet is still hungry at mealtime; willingly tries new foods and enjoys cooking.

■ Prefers certain favorite foods, usually pizza, ice cream, cake, and cookies; has few dislikes, but tends not to be fond of cooked vegetables.

■ Battles with parents over posture and table manners (elbows on the table; slouched in chair; fisted grasp of forks and spoons), but usually displays good manners at friends' houses.

Toileting, Bathing, Dressing

■ Shows little interest in personal hygiene; often needs reminders to bathe, wash hair, brush teeth, put on clean clothes.

■ Requires coaxing to bathe, but once bath is started getting them out may be difficult.

■ Shows some interest in appearance; wants to dress and look like friends; school clothes take on an important role in self-identification.

■ Manages own toileting needs without reminders; seldom gets up at night unless too much liquid is consumed before bedtime.

Sleeping

■ Seems unaware of fatigue and the need for sleep.

■ Requires nine to ten hours of sleep to function throughout the day; goes to bed around 8:30 or 9:30 P.M., wakes up around 7 A.M. without much trouble.

■ Girls may have more bedtime rituals and take longer to fall asleep than do boys.

■ Nightmares and fears of the dark may redevelop; some children experience sleepwalking, waking up in the middle of the night, or bedwetting. Parents should not criticize children who are experiencing these problems and seek professional help if they persist.

Play and Social Activities

■ Maintains activity level that fluctuates between extremes of high intensity and almost nonexistent activity; may virtually collapse following periods of intense play.

■ Spends free time reading magazines, playing computer games, watching videos, and talking with friends.

■ Likes to form and join clubs with secret codes, languages, and signs.

■ Offers to help with simple household chores, such as dusting and sweeping, vacuuming, and putting away groceries.

■ Develops new hobbies or collections based on special interests.

Learning Activities

Tips for parents and teachers:

■ Take advantage of educational opportunities in the community: plan field trips to the beach, farmers' market, library, museum, park, garden center, cabinet maker, or grocery store.

■ Encourage children to appreciate diversity by learning about the customs and celebrations of other cultures. Obtain library books, visit Web sites, invite guests, locate musical instruments, and prepare various ethnic foods. Teach children to be accepting and avoid prejudice through your own actions and words.

■ Gather sports equipment, such as balls, bats, nets, and rackets; encourage children to organize and participate in group activities.

■ Provide space, seeds, and tools for planting and maintaining a garden.

■ Assemble materials and provide basic instructions for conducting science experiments; science activity suggestions can be found in many good books at the public library or on child-oriented Web sites.

■ Nurture children's interest in reading, writing, and friendships by locating pen pals in another state or country; encourage children to write back and forth (via letter or e-mail), read books about where the pen pal lives, and locate the state or country on a map.

Developmental Alerts

Check with a health care provider or early childhood specialist if, by the eleventh birthday, the child *does not*:

■ Continue to grow at a rate appropriate for the child's gender.

- Show continued improvement of fine motor skills.

- Make or keep friends.

- Enjoy going to school and show interest in learning (have children's hearing and vision tested; vision and hearing problems affect children's ability to learn and their interest in learning).

- Approach new situations with reasonable confidence.

- Handle failure and frustration in a constructive manner.

- Sleep through the night or experiences prolonged problems with bedwetting, nightmares, or sleepwalking.

Safety Concerns

Continue to implement Safety Concerns described for the previous stages. Be aware of new safety issues as the child continues to grow and develop:

Media Exposure

- Be aware of on-line sites that children visit; check the nature of information available on these sites.

- Know what video games children play and determine if they expose children to violence.

Firearms

- Educate children about the dangers of guns and other weapons.

- Store firearms and ammunition separately and keep in locked storage.

- Never leave loaded firearms unattended.

Traffic

- Insist that children wear seat belts on every motor trip.

- Review safe practices for crossing streets, getting in and out of parked cars, riding a bicycle, skateboarding, and otherwise acting responsibly around traffic.

Figure 8-5 Eleven- and twelve-year-olds enjoy participating in
sports and organized activities.

 # Eleven- and Twelve-Year-Olds

For the most part, eleven- and twelve-year-olds are enduring individuals. They are curious, energetic, helpful, and happy. They help with chores around the house, sometimes even volunteering before being asked. Their language, motor, and cognitive skills are reaching adult levels of sophistication. By age twelve, children have developed a sense of confidence in their capabilities and approach tasks with renewed interest. Their emotional stability is generally smoother, and they encounter fewer conflicts with parents and peers. Eleven- and twelve-year-olds enjoy participating in organized sports and physical activity; Figure 8-5. In general, their health is good, and they begin to understand that a healthy lifestyle is not only important, but takes regular work and effort. However, they also see themselves as invincible. Few children believe they will ever experience serious health conditions, such as lung cancer, diabetes, or heart disease, despite engaging in risky behaviors (e.g., smoking, following a sedentary lifestyle, eating a high-fat diet).

11- & 12-Year-Olds

Developmental Profiles
and Growth Patterns

Growth and Physical Characteristics

■ Height and weight vary significantly from child to child; body shape and proportion are influenced by heredity and environment; birth length is tripled by the end of this period.

■ Girls are first to experience a prepuberty growth spurt, growing taller and weighing more than boys at this age; may gain as much as 3.5 inches (8.75 cm) and 20 pounds (44 kg) in one year; this period of rapid growth ends around age twelve for girls; boys' growth is much slower.

■ Bodily changes mark approaching puberty: widening hips and budding breasts (girls), enlarging testes and penis (boys), appearance of pubic hair.

■ Menstruation may begin if it has not already started; some girls have vaginal discharge sooner; may be upset if not progressing at the same rate as friends.

■ Spontaneous erections are common among eleven- and twelve-year-old boys; pictures, physical activity, talk, and daydreams can trigger these events; some will begin ejaculating seminal fluid.

■ Muscle mass and strength increase, especially in boys; girls often reach their maximum muscle strength by age twelve years.

■ Posture is more erect; increases in bone size and length cause shoulders, collarbone, rib cage, and shoulder blades to appear more prominent.

■ Complaints of headaches and blurred vision are not uncommon if experiencing vision problems; added strain of schoolwork (smaller print, computer use, intense writing) may cause some children to request an eye examination.

Motor Development

■ Displays movements that are smoother and more coordinated; however, rapid growth spurts may cause temporary clumsiness.

■ Enjoys participation in activities, such as dancing, karate, soccer, gymnastics, swimming, or organized games where improved skills can be used and tested.

■ Concentrates efforts on continued refinement of fine motor abilities through a variety of activities: model-building, rocket construction, drawing, woodworking, cooking, sewing, arts and crafts, writing letters, or playing an instrument; has now perfected all fundamental gross motor skills.

■ Requires outlets for release of excess energy that builds during the school day; enjoys team sports, riding bikes, playing in the park, taking dance lessons, going for a walk with friends.

■ Has an abundance of energy, but also fatigues quickly.

■ Uses improved strength to run faster, throw balls farther, jump higher, kick or bat balls more accurately, and wrestle with friends.

11- & 12-Year-Olds

Figure 8-6 Enjoys researching and solving problems.

Perceptual-Cognitive Development

- Begins thinking in more abstract terms; expanded memory ability enables improved long-term recall; now remembers stored information, so no longer must rely solely on experiencing an event in order to understand it.
- Succeeds in sequencing, ordering, and classifying because of improved long-term memory capacity; these are skills needed for solving complex math problems.
- Accepts the idea that problems can have multiple solutions; often works through problems by talking aloud to self.
- Enjoys challenges, problem-solving, researching, and testing possible solutions; researches encyclopedias, the Internet, and dictionaries for information; Figure 8-6.
- Exhibits longer attention span; stays focused on completing school assignments and other tasks.
- Develops detailed plans and lists to reach a desired goal.
- Performs many routine tasks without having to think; increased memory sophistication makes automatic responses possible.
- Shows more complex understanding of cause and effect; identifies factors that may have contributed to, or caused an event: combining baking soda with vinegar releases a gas.

Speech and Language Development

■ Completes the majority of language development by the end of this stage; only subtle refinements are still necessary during the next few years.

■ Loves to talk and argue, often nonstop, with anyone who will listen.

■ Uses longer and more complex sentence structures.

■ Masters increasingly complex vocabulary; adds 4,000 to 5,000 new words each year; uses vocabulary skillfully to weave elaborate stories and precise descriptions.

■ Becomes a thoughtful listener.

■ Understands that words and statements may have implied (intended) meanings: when your mother asks, "Is your homework done?" she really means you'd better stop playing, gather up your books, and get started.

■ Grasps concepts of irony and sarcasm; has a good sense of humor and enjoys telling jokes, riddles, and rhymes to entertain others.

■ Masters several language styles, shifting back and forth based on the occasion: a more formal style when talking with teachers, a more casual style with parents, a style that often includes slang and code words when conversing with friends.

Personal-Social Development

■ Delights in organizing group games, but may modify rules while game is in progress.

■ Views self-image as very important; typically defines self in terms of appearance, possessions, or activities; may also make comparisons to admired adults.

■ Becomes increasingly self-conscious and self-focused; understands the need to assume responsibility for own behavior and that there are consequences associated with one's actions.

■ Begins to think and talk about occupational choices and career plans; daydreams and fantasizes about the future.

■ Develops a critical and idealistic view of the world; realizes the world is larger than one's own neighborhood; expresses interest in other cultures, foods, languages, and customs; Figure 8-7.

■ Adapts dress, hair styles, and mannerisms of popular sports figures and celebrities.

■ Recognizes that loyalty, honesty, trustworthiness, and being a good listener are prerequisites to becoming a good friend; spends more time now with peers than with parents or siblings.

■ Handles frustration with fewer emotional outbursts; is able to discuss what is emotionally troubling; accompanies words with facial expressions and gestures for emphasis.

Figure 8-7 Expresses interest in other cultures, customs, and foods.

Daily Routines

Eleven- and Twelve-Year-Olds

Eating

■ Eats nonstop and is always hungry; boys in particular may consume astonishing amounts and combinations of food. Boys require approximately 2,500 calories daily; girls need 2,200.

■ Has few dislikes; willing to eat less preferred foods now and then; shows interest in trying foods from other cultures.

■ Needs big snack upon arriving home from school; searches cabinets and refrigerator for anything to eat.

■ Makes connection between eating (calories) and gaining or losing weight, especially girls; for example, some girls may talk about dieting.

Toileting, Bathing, Dressing

■ Cares for most personal needs without adult assistance.
■ Enjoys bathing and keeping self clean; often prefers taking showers.
■ Still may need occasional reminder to wash hands.
■ Brushes and flosses teeth willingly; a bright smile is important for appearance. Dental checkups, every six months, are needed to monitor rapidly erupting permanent teeth and treat cavities; many children already have several decayed or filled teeth.
■ Takes pride in appearance; likes to wear what is fashionable or what friends are wearing.

Sleeping

■ Needs plenty of sleep; growth spurts and active play often leave children feeling tired.
■ Heads to bed without much resistance, but now wants to stay up until 9 or 10 P.M., even later on weekends and nonschool days.
■ Sleeps less soundly than previously; may wake up early and read or finish homework before getting up.
■ Bad dreams still trouble some eleven- and twelve-year-olds.

Play and Social Activities

■ Shows less interest in frivolous play; prefers goal-directed activities: money-making schemes, competing on a swim team, writing newsletters, attending summer camp.
■ Prefers involvement in organized groups, such as sports teams, 4-H Club, Scouts, or just spending time alone with a friend; never without something to do.
■ Likes animals; offers to care for, and train, pets.
■ Reads enthusiastically; enjoys listening to music, attending movies, watching the news, surfing on the computer, and playing video games.
■ Enjoys outdoor activities, such as skateboarding, roller blading, basketball, riding bikes, or walking with friends.

 *Learning Activities*

Tips for parents and teachers:

■ Encourage children's interest in reading; take them to the library or book mobile.

■ Read and discuss newspaper and magazine articles together; suggest that children create their own newsletter.

- Help children develop a sense of responsibility by assigning tasks they can perform on a regular basis: caring for a pet, reading stories to a younger sibling, folding laundry, loading the dishwasher, washing dishes, sweeping the garage.

- Gather a variety of large cardboard boxes, paints, and other materials; challenge children to design a structure with them: a town, train, castle, farm, puppet theater.

- Help children stage a play; invite them to write the script, design scenery, construct simple props, and rehearse.

- Offer to help children plan and organize a pet show, bike parade, or scavenger hunt.

- Locate free or low-cost opportunities to join organized group or sporting activities; these are often available through local parks and recreation departments, YMCA/YWCAs, church youth groups, and after-school programs.

- Provide children with a variety of art materials: paints, crayons, markers, paper, old magazines and catalogues, cloth scraps; encourage children to collect natural materials, such as leaves, pebbles, interesting twigs, seed pods, feathers, and grasses to use for artistic collages.

Developmental Alerts

Check with a health care provider or early childhood specialist if, by the thirteenth birthday, the child *does not*:

- Have movements that are smooth and coordinated.

- Have energy sufficient for playing, riding bikes, or engaging in other desired activities.

- Stay focused on tasks at hand.

- Understand basic cause-and-effect relationships.

- Handle criticism and frustration with a reasonable response (physical aggression and excessive crying could be an indication of other, underlying problems).

- Exhibit a healthy appetite (frequent skipping of meals is not typical for this age group).

- Make and keep friends.

Safety Concerns

Continue to implement Safety Concerns described for the previous stages. Be aware of new safety issues as the child continues to grow and develop:

Machinery

■ Teach children how to operate small appliances or school machinery safely.

■ Provide basic first aid instruction for responding to injuries.

Sports

■ Make sure proper protective equipment is available and worn; check its condition periodically.

■ Provide instruction, or make sure an adult is supervising any competition; check safety of area and equipment.

Substance Abuse

■ Be aware of warning signs associated with "huffing" (inhaling) hazardous vapors from common household products, such as hair spray, polish remover, aerosol paints, fabric protector. Note unusual odor on children's breath or clothing, slurred speech, jitteriness, poor appetite, bloodshot eyes, or reddened areas around nose or mouth.

Water

■ Provide, and require, children to wear flotation devices whenever fishing, skiing, or boating.

■ Teach basic water safety and make sure children learn how to swim.

SUMMARY

Growth patterns during this stage are irregular and inconsistent. Girls tend to grow more than boys, with fairly significant variations occurring from child to child. Most children are rather carefree, happy, energetic, industrious, and eager to learn. They spend the years between ages nine and twelve fine-tuning basic skills, many of which were already in place. Advanced cognitive abilities continue to emerge, enabling children to think in the abstract, understand concepts of weight, distance, and time, follow detailed instructions, and comprehend cause-and-effect relation-

11- & 12-Year-Olds

ships. Feelings related to self-concept gradually shift from overly harsh self-criticism to gaining confidence in one's abilities. Although friends and friendships are very important, family ties are still valued. Participation in group activities and team sports provides a necessary outlet for excess energy, competition, development of advanced motor skills, and companionship.

 KEY TERMS

concrete operational thought   logic

intuition

APPLY YOUR KNOWLEDGE

A. Apply What You Have Learned

Reread the developmental sketch about Juan and Carlin at the beginning of the chapter. How might you answer the following questions?

1. Would you consider Carlin's development to be typical for a nine-year-old?

2. Would it be developmentally appropriate to expect most eleven-year-olds to like school?

3. Why should Carlin's lack of friends be of concern?

4. From a developmental perspective, do you think Juan's reactions to having his sister tag along are typical or atypical? Explain.

5. What physical characteristics would you expect to observe in the "average" eleven-year-old?

6. Which of Carlin's behaviors would cause you to recommend referral to an early childhood specialist for additional evaluation? Explain.

B. Review Questions

1. List three speech-language skills that are characteristic of most nine- and ten-year-olds.

2. List two changes in growth which typically occur in:
   a. Nine- to ten-year-olds
   b. Eleven- to twelve-year-olds

3. List two characteristics that describe the cognitive development of most eleven- and twelve-year-olds.

4. List three qualities that are needed in order to make and keep friends.

HELPFUL WEB SITES

After School	http://www.afterschool.gov
Canadian Parents Online	http://www.canadianparents.com/schoolaged
ERIC Clearinghouse on Teaching & Teacher Education	http://www.ericsp.org
National Network for Child Care	http://www.nncc.org/SACC/devapprop
National Parent Information Center	http://www.npin.org
Teacher Pathfinder	http://www.teacherpathfinder.org

For additional child development resources, visit our Web site www.earlychilded.delmar.com

Chapter

9

When and Where to Seek Help

 OBJECTIVES

After reading this chapter, you should be able to:

- List five or more features of federal legislation enacted on behalf of children with exceptionalities and their families beginning in the mid-1960s.
- Explain both the purpose of developmental screening tests and the reasons for exercising caution when interpreting results.
- Describe several factors that complicate the developmental picture when deciding whether or not a child is developing normally.
- Defend this statement: observing and recording a child's behaviors is an essential first step in determining if there is a developmental problem.
- Explain why a Family Service Coordinator is essential to successful implementation of intervention recommendations for child and family.

 MEET ANDREY AND HIS MOTHER

Andrey, at four years, nine months of age, was new to the Head Start class in the urban area where his family was now living. His teachers were soon concerned about his overall development. He seemed unable to follow directions, his language skills appeared to be limited, and his speech was unintelligible to everyone but family. When trying to interact with other children, he frequently hit them, apparently to gain their attention. During entire free play periods, he seemed incapable of playing with a specific toy or child for longer than two or

Figure 9-1 Parents often wonder if their child is developing "normally."

three minutes at a time. There was one exception: block building held his attention for fifteen minutes and more. When asked about Andrey's health history, his mother spoke vaguely of earaches and runny ears, "hot spells," and "twitches." At age twenty-one, Andrey's mother had had ten years of special education. She was a thin, pale woman, midway into her third pregnancy. Working part-time as a waitress, she often was the only breadwinner, as the father, a year older than she, was frequently unemployed. She expressed warmth and concern for Andrey and his two-year-old sister, but apparently had never understood the importance of medical care or nutrition for herself or her children. It appeared that she had been unable to follow through on whatever medical assistance she had been offered. The fact that the family had moved seven times since Andrey was born quite likely accounted, in part, for the family having fallen through the cracks of the social service system.

Is my child all right? Most parents, at one time or another, ask this question during their child's infancy and growing-up years; Figure 9-1. Many caregivers and teachers ask a similar question about a child who seems somehow "different" from other children with whom they work. Such questions are a positive sign; they indicate awareness and concern. Children, as emphasized in Chapter 1, vary greatly in their development. It is the rare child who is truly typical in every way. Many children with developmental irregularities of one kind or another experience no long-term negative effects. Other children with irregularities that appear no more threatening may be at developmental risk. In both instances the child needs to be seen by a physician and perhaps referred for additional services.

PUBLIC POLICY AND SOCIAL ATTITUDES

Supporting optimum development in infants and children has become a major social and legislative focus of society. Much of the initial impetus came in the 1960s as one aspect of the anti-poverty movement (often referred to as the *War on Poverty*). Many precedent-setting research studies provided conclusive evidence that we could significantly reduce developmental disabilities in infants and children. Consequently, several major strategies have evolved. One is based on prevention of atypical development. Another is the early identification of children with, or at-risk for, developmental problems. If a potential problem is identified, the next step is providing an intervention program as soon as feasible, thus minimizing the effects of the problem on a child's overall development. Throughout this process a critical factor is supporting the child's family by helping them to understand and participate in the intervention recommendations.

Legislation Supporting Optimum Development

Beginning in the mid-1960s, several pieces of legislation led to the implementation of programs for supporting child and family health and reducing developmental risks. Head Start (PL 88-452; 1965) was the first such law to be funded. It was soon followed by Early and Periodic Screening, Diagnosis and Treatment, (EPSDT) (1967). The Supplemental Nutrition Program for Women, Infants, and Children (WIC), another such legislative act, was mandated in 1972.

In the late 1960s came legislation related to children who were developmentally different. The Handicapped Children's Early Education and Assistance Act (HCEEAA) was authorized in 1968. In 1975, The Education for all Handicapped Children Act (EHA) was passed and later renamed Education of Individuals with Disabilities Act (IDEA; 1997). (See Appendix 7 for summary statements of the acts.)

Early Identification and Intervention Programs

As a result of legislation and changes in public policy, several avenues are now available for getting children with suspected developmental problems into appropriate evaluation and intervention programs.

Infants and Children at Medical Risk

Knowledge of medical conditions that might be associated with developmental difficulties is growing rapidly in the medical community. Family physicians and pediatricians are becoming increasingly aware of physical characteristics in infants that might indicate the presence of one of a multitude of syndromes that have been identified in the recent decades. Physicians also are becoming increasingly knowledgeable about neurological development in infancy and are better able to detect worrisome deviations. Referral to genetic and neurological specialists often leads to early detection of medical conditions associated with high risk of developmental delays.

Another group of children at medical risk for developmental problems includes infants discharged from premature nurseries and neonatal intensive care units. Many communities in urban areas now have follow-up clinics for this high-risk group of infants. Children with suspect development are typically referred to intervention programs from such settings.

Community Screening

The majority of young children who will benefit from early identification and intervention do not come always from medically high-risk groups. These children may be best located through community screening services.

Screening programs are designed to identify children who have or may be at-risk for developmental problems. Primarily, the focus is on hearing and vision, general health, and overall development; Figure 9-2. Screening tests are designed to be easily administered so that large numbers of children can be assessed in their own communities through public health departments, Head Start programs, or child care centers. Without early screening, many children may not receive necessary services until they reach school age. By that time, if there is a problem, it often has become serious, requiring extensive therapy and special education.

Child Find is a nationwide screening program with the goal of locating infants and children who have undiagnosed developmental problems or are at-risk for the onset of such problems. This federally funded program has two major purposes. One is to identify eligible children as early in life as possible in order to provide diagnostic services. The second is to help families locate appropriate intervention programs and services. Each state is required, by law, to establish a Child Find system.

Child Find—a screening program designed to locate children with developmental problems through improved public awareness.

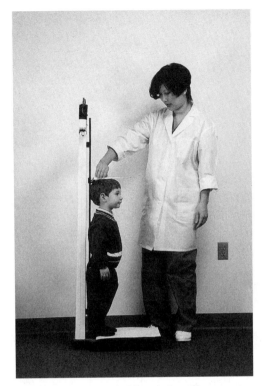

Figure 9-2 Assessing children's health is an important component of developmental screening.

IS THERE A PROBLEM?

Deciding if a developmental delay or irregularity is of serious concern may not be easy. The signs can be so subtle, so hard to pinpoint, that it is often difficult to distinguish clearly between children who definitely have a problem, the definite *yes's*, and those who definitely do not have a problem, the definite *no's*. Identifying the *maybe's*—is there or is there not a problem—can be an even more complex issue.

In determining if a delay or deviation is of real concern, several factors may complicate the matter. For example:

■ Children who exhibit signs of developmental problems in certain areas often continue to develop like a typical child in every other way; such children present a confusing developmental profile. (See, Developmental Checklists, Appendix 3).

■ Great variation exists in the range of an individual child's achievements within developmental areas. The rate of maturation is uneven, and conditions in the

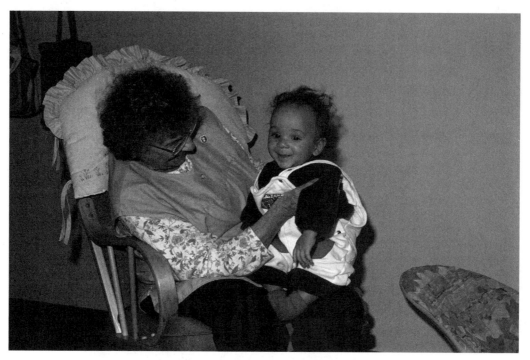

Figure 9-3 Diversity of family and community values, beliefs,
and cultural differences must be considered and treated with respect and dignity.

child's environment are continually changing. Both maturation and environment interact to exert a strong influence on every aspect of development.

■ Family beliefs, values, and cultural background have significant influence on how parents raise their children. Developmental milestones are not universal; how they are perceived varies from culture to culture, even from family to family. Respect for diverse family and community lifestyles is always a consideration when gathering and interpreting information about a child's development; Figure 9-3. (See diversity insert.)

■ Developmental delays or problems may not be immediately apparent. Many children learn to compensate for a deficiency, such as a mild to moderate vision or hearing loss. Sometimes deficiencies do not become obvious until the child is placed in structured and more demanding situations (as in a first-grade reading class).

■ Intermittent health problems can affect children's performance. For example, a child may have severe and recurring bouts of otitis media that appear to clear up completely between episodes. A hearing test administered when the child is free of infection may reveal no hearing loss, while the same child may be quite deaf when the infection is active. Intermittent periods of near-deafness, sometimes lasting a week or more, can result in language and cognitive delays, and even in severely challenging behaviors in some children.

When to Seek Help

At what point should a hunch or uncomfortable feeling about a child be a call for action? The answer is clear: whenever parents or teachers feel uncertain about a child's development or behavior. Any such uneasiness needs to be discussed with a pediatrician or other health care provider. Working together, a determination can be made regarding the need for developmental screening.

Concern about a developmental irregularity demands investigation whenever it interferes with a child's participation in everyday activities. The frequent occurrence or constant repetition of a troublesome behavior is a reliable sign that professional help should be sought. Seldom is a single incidence of a questionable behavior cause for concern. What is of concern, however, is a child's *continuing* reluctance to attempt a new skill or to acquire fully a basic developmental skill. For example, a ten-month-old who tries to sit alone but still must use both hands for support may or may not have a problem. On the other hand, clusters of developmental differences are always significant: a ten-month-old who is not sitting without support, not smiling, and not babbling in response to others is likely to be at developmental risk.

What do teachers and caregivers do when a parent fails to express concern or denies the possibility of a problem? Although it may be difficult, it is the staff's responsibility to discuss their concerns in a conference with the parents. In that setting, every effort must be made to be straightforward and to help parents accept that the child should be referred for evaluation. Under no circumstances may staff members bypass parents and do the referring themselves. Staff must, however, reassure parents of their willingness to assist in finding the necessary services.

INFORMATION GATHERING

Several levels of information gathering must be included in a developmental evaluation: observation and recording, screening, and diagnostic assessment. Diagnostic assessment includes in-depth testing and clinical interpretation of results. Clinicians from various disciplines should participate in the diagnosis. It is their responsibility to provide detailed information about the specific nature of the child's problems. For example, a four-year-old's delayed speech may be observed by parents and noted during routine screening procedures. Subsequent diagnostic testing by clinicians may pinpoint several other conditions: a moderate, **bilateral** hearing loss, poor production of many letter sounds, and an expressive vocabulary typical of a three-year-old. These clinical findings can be translated into educational strategies and intervention procedures that will benefit the child's overall development.

Observing and Recording

The evaluation process always begins with systematic observation. (See observation insert.) Noting and recording various aspects of a child's behavior enables the evaluator, whether parent, teacher, or clinician, to focus on what is actually occurring. In other words, observations provide information about what the child can and cannot do at the time of the observation.

Direct observation often confirms or rules out impressions or suspicions regarding a child's abilities. For example, a child may not count to 5 when asked to do so in a testing situation. That same child, however, may be observed to count seven or eight objects spontaneously and correctly while at play. A child thought to be hyperactive may be observed to sit quietly for five to ten minutes when given more interesting and challenging activities, thereby ruling out hyperactivity. *Note:* The term *hyperactive* is greatly overused and misused. A child should not be so labeled unless specifically diagnosed by a multidisciplinary team. Focusing on a child at play, alone or with other children, is especially revealing. No evaluation is valid without direct observations of a child in familiar surroundings.

Parents' observations are particularly valuable; Figure 9-4. They provide information and understanding that cannot be obtained from any other source. Their observations also give insight into family attitudes, perceptions, and expectations concerning the child. Involving parents in the observation phase of evaluation may also help reduce their anxiety. Furthermore, direct observation often points up unrecognized strengths and abilities. When parents actually see their child engaged in appropriate activities, it may encourage them to focus more on the child's strengths instead of limitations.

Screening Tests

In addition to direct observation, screening tests are an important step in identifying developmental problems. The purpose of these tests is to determine if the child needs a more comprehensive evaluation. Screening tests are designed to appraise general abilities as well as impairments or delays in fine and gross motor skills, cognition, speech and language development, and personal and social responsiveness.

---

bilateral—affecting both sides, as in loss of hearing in both ears.

Figure 9-4 Parents can provide important information about their child's development.

If problems or suspected problems are noted during screening, further in-depth clinical assessment is needed before a final diagnosis can be reached. *Note:* Results obtained from screening tests are neither conclusive nor diagnostic. They do not predict a child's future abilities or achievement potential, and should not be used as a basis for planning intervention programs.

Several questions should be asked when choosing or interpreting a screening instrument:

■ Is it appropriate for the child's age?
■ Is it free of bias related to the child's economic, geographic, or cultural background?
■ Can it be administered in the child's first language? If not, is a skilled interpreter available to assist the child and family?
■ Is it reliable in separating children who should be referred for further testing from those who should not?

Appendix 5 provides a sampling of widely used screening tests and a brief list of popular assessment instruments. Included are examples of ecological evaluations of home and school; information about the child's everyday surroundings is essential in planning both prevention and intervention programs.

Interpreting Screening Results. The widespread use of screening programs is of great benefit in detecting possible developmental problems, but the findings are always open to question. The screening process itself may have a negative effect on the outcome. Children's attention spans, especially those of young children, often are short and vary considerably from day to day and from task to task. Illness, fatigue, anxiety, lack of cooperation, irritability, or restlessness can have a negative effect. Poor performance may also result when children are unaccustomed to being tested or unfamiliar with the person doing the testing. Often children are capable of doing much better in a familiar setting. Consequently, results derived from screening assessments must be regarded with caution. The following points are intended as reminders for both parents and teachers.

■ Avoid conclusions based on limited information or a single test score. The results may not be an accurate representation of the child's actual development or developmental potential. Only repeated and periodic observation can provide a complete picture of the child's developing abilities.

■ Never underestimate the influence of home and family on a child's performance. Newer screening procedures make a greater effort to promote family participation and to evaluate family concerns, priorities, and resources. There also is growing emphasis on screening in familiar environments and everyday situations where children feel more secure.

■ Recognize the dangers of labeling a child as learning disabled, mentally retarded, or behavior-disordered, especially on the basis of any one test. Labels are of little benefit, and too often have a negative effect on expectations for both the child and the way parents and teachers respond to the child.

■ Question test scores. Test results can easily be misinterpreted. One test may suggest that a child has a developmental delay when actually nothing is wrong. Such conclusions are called *false positives*. The opposite conclusion can also be reached. A child may have a problem that does not show up in the screening process and so may be incorrectly identified as normal. This is a *false negative*. The first situation leads to unnecessary anxiety and disappointment, and may change the way the family responds to their child. The latter situation, the false negative, can lull a family into not seeking further help, and so the child's problem worsens. Both situations can be avoided with careful interpretation of test scores.

■ Understand that results from screening tests *do not* constitute a diagnosis. Additional information must be collected and in-depth clinical testing completed before a diagnosis is given or confirmed. Even then, errors may occur. There are many reasons for misdiagnosis, such as inconsistent and rapid changes in a child's growth or changing environmental factors such as divorce or family relocation.

- Do not use failed items on a screening test as curriculum items or skills to be taught; a test item is simply one isolated example of a broad range of skills to be expected in a given developmental area at an approximate age. A child who cannot stand on one foot for five seconds will not overcome a developmental problem by being taught to stand on one foot for a given time period. *Screening test items are not a suitable basis for constructing curriculum activities.*
- Recognize that test results do not predict the child's developmental future, nor do they necessarily correlate with subsequent testing. There is always the need for *ongoing* observation, assessment, and in-depth clinical diagnosis when screening tests indicate potential problems and delays.

IQ Tests: Are They Appropriate for Young Children?

Intelligence tests, such as the Wechsler Intelligence Scale for Children (WISC) and the Stanford Binet Intelligence Scales, were not designed or intended to be used as screening instruments. Neither are they regarded by most early childhood specialists as appropriate to use with young children for any purpose. IQ tests administered during the early years are not valid predictors of future or even current intellectual performance. Especially, they do not predict subsequent academic performance. (The single best predictor of a child's school achievements is the level of the mother's education!) IQ tests do not take into account opportunities the child has had to learn, the quality of those learning experiences, or what the *dominant culture* says a child should know at a given age. Children raised in poverty, for example, or in non-English-speaking homes, often do not have the same opportunities to acquire specific kinds of information represented by the test items. Therefore, an IQ test score, used as the sole determinant of a child's cognitive or intellectual development, must be challenged.

Achievement Tests

In primary, elementary, and high school, achievement tests tend to be administered regularly by many school districts; Figure 9-5. These tests are designed to measure how much the child has been learning in school about specific subject areas. Depending on the results, each child is assigned a percentile ranking, based on a comparison with other children of the same grade level. For example, a child in the 50th percentile in math is doing as well as 50 percent of the children in the same grade. Again, test scores should be backed up by teachers' observations of children and by collected samples (portfolios) of children's work.

---

achievement tests—tests used to measure a child's academic progress (what has been learned).

Figure 9-5 Achievement tests are often administered to assess student learning.

DIAGNOSIS AND REFERRAL

Information obtained from direct observations of the child combined with the screening test results provide the basis for the next question: Are comprehensive diagnostic procedures required? Not all children will need an in-depth clinical assessment, but many will, if they and their family are to receive the best possible referral for intervention services. Diagnoses and referrals are most effective when based on a team process that combines the input of clinicians and family.

The Developmental Team

Federal law requires that parents be involved in all phases of the assessment and intervention process. Working in collaboration with professionals, parents become important members of the child's **developmental team**. A family-centered approach

---

developmental team—a team of qualified professionals such as special educators, speech pathologists, occupational therapists, social workers, audiologists, nurses, and physical therapists, who evaluate a child's developmental progress and, together, prepare an intervention plan that addresses the child's special needs.

improves the sharing of information, and enables parents to learn and implement therapy recommendations at home. Sustained interest and participation in the child's intervention program can be achieved when the developmental team:

- keeps parents informed
- explains rationales for treatment procedures
- emphasizes the child's progress
- teaches parents how to work with their child at home
- provides parents with positive feedback for their continuing efforts and advocacy on their child's behalf

In managing developmental disorders, best practice suggests that the pooling of knowledge and multidisciplinary expertise is required—in other words, a team approach. For example, team effort provides the most accurate picture of how a delay in one area can affect development in other areas, just as progress in one area supports progress in others. A two-year-old with a hearing loss could experience delays in language, as well as cognitive and social development. Thus, appropriate intervention strategies for this child may require the services of an audiologist, speech and language therapist, early childhood teacher, nurse, and, perhaps, social worker. If a team approach is to benefit the child's overall development, effective communication and cooperation among specialists, service providers, and the family is essential. This process is facilitated by the inclusion of an Individual Family Service Plan (IFSP for infants and toddlers) or an Individualized Educational Plan (IEP for preschool through school age).

Family Service Coordinator

For many families, the process of approaching multiple agencies and dealing with bureaucratic red tape is overwhelming. As a result, these families often do not, or cannot, complete the necessary arrangements unless they receive assistance and ongoing support. The role of a **Family Service Coordinator** is so crucial to successful intervention that it has been written into federal legislation (PL 99-457) to help families deal with their children's developmental problems. A Family Service Coordinator works closely with the family, matching their needs with service agencies and educational programs in the community. The coordinator also assists the family in establishing initial contacts and making final arrangements.

Family Service Coordinator—an individual who serves as a family's advocate and assists them with identifying, locating, and making final arrangements with community services.

Figure 9-6 Information gathered through teacher observations provides valuable insight about children's developmental progress.

Referral

The referral process involves a multiple-step approach. As described earlier, the child's strengths, weaknesses, and developmental skills are evaluated. The family's needs and resources (such as financial, psychological, physical, and transportation capabilities) must also be taken into consideration. For example, if a family cannot afford special services, has no knowledge of financial assistance programs, and does not own a car, it is unlikely that they will be able to follow up on professional recommendations. However, such problems are seldom insurmountable. Most communities have individuals and social service agencies available to help families locate and utilize needed services.

Placement in an appropriate educational setting is frequently recommended as part of the intervention plan. In these settings, classroom teachers and other members of the developmental team conduct ongoing assessments of the child's progress; Figure 9-6. In addition, the developmental team reviews the appropriateness of both the placement and the special services on a regular basis to determine if the child's and family's needs are being met. This step is especially critical with infants and toddlers, whose development progresses quickly. Throughout, there must be continuing communication and support among teachers, practitioners, and parents to ensure that the child is receiving individually appropriate as well as maximum benefits from the prescribed program.

 ## SUMMARY

Beginning in the mid-1960s, a series of federal laws changed public attitudes and policies related to persons with developmental disabilities. Several of the laws focus on infants and children with, or at-risk for, developmental problems. Mandated specifically are programs concerned with prevention, early identification, and intervention where there is an obvious or potential problem. The role of the family is formally recognized as essential when addressing the child's needs as is the clinical expertise from a variety of disciplines. Integral to the parent–team collaboration is a designated *Family Service Coordinator* who orchestrates child, family, and team members' needs, concerns, and recommendations.

Any concern about a child's development demands immediate attention. The starting point is firsthand observation of the child in a familiar, everyday environment. One or more screening tests, appropriate to the child's age, language, and culture, can be administered concurrently. Results from a single test may be misleading; more than one screening instrument should be administered, and all results call for cautious interpretation. In-depth clinical diagnosis is the next step if observation and screening results indicate the likelihood of a problem. Therapeutic intervention for infants, toddlers, and preschoolers often includes placement in an early education program. Regardless of the child's age, it is intended that a Family Service Coordinator work with the child, family, and school on an ongoing basis as needed, until the child reaches eighteen years of age.

KEY TERMS

achievement tests

bilateral

Child Find

developmental team

Family Service Coordinator

APPLY YOUR KNOWLEDGE

A. Apply What You Have Learned

1. What were some of the specific behaviors that Andrey's teachers were concerned about that led them to suspect that he might be at-risk developmentally?

2. Prior to holding a first conference with Andrey's mother, what kinds of information do teachers need to record through direct observation of Andrey in the classroom?

3. In the teachers' initial evaluation of Andrey's overall development, why is it imperative that there be a series of firsthand observations and note-taking on him in a familiar setting such as the classroom and play yard?

4. Describe the three pieces of legislation discussed in the chapter (and more fully described in Appendix 7) that could be of benefit to a high-risk family like Andrey's.

5. What role and what kinds of help might a Family Service Coordinator provide for Andrey's family?

B. Review Questions

1. List three concerns that may prevent parents from seeking help for their child.

2. Describe three qualities that should be considered when deciding if a screening test is appropriate for young children.

3. List three methods that a developmental team can use to foster family involvement.

4. Identify and discuss three reasons why it is important to foster family involvement in a child's intervention program.

5. List three aspects of early development that can make it difficult to pinpoint a potential problem.

6. Describe three reasons why the results of screening tests should be interpreted with caution.

For additional child development resources, visit our Web site www.earlychilded.delmar.com

Summary of Reflexes

Age	Appears	Disappears
Birth	swallow*, gag*, cough*, yawn*, blink suck rooting Moro (startle) grasp stepping plantar elimination tonic neck reflex (TNR)	
1–4 months	Landau tear* (cries with tears)	grasp suck (becomes voluntary) step root tonic neck reflex (TNR)
4–8 months	parachute palmar grasp pincer grasp	Moro (startle)
8–12 months		palmar grasp plantar reflex
12–18 months		
18–24 months		Landau
3–4 years		parachute elimination (becomes voluntary)

*Permanent; present throughout person's lifetime.

2

Recommended Immunization Schedule

Recommended Childhood Immunization Schedule

Vaccines are listed under routinely recommended ages. [Bars] indicate range of recommended ages fore immunization. Any dose not given at the recommended age should be given as a "catch-up" immunization at any subsequent visit when indicated and feasible. (Ovals) indicate vaccines to be given if previously recommended doses were missed or given earlier than the recommended minimum age.

	Birth	1 month	2 months	4 months	6 months	12 months	15 months	18 months	4-6 years	11-12 years	14-16 years
Hepatitis B	Hep B	Hep B				Hep B				(Hep B)	
Diphtheria, Tetanus, Pertussis			DTaP	DTaP	DTaP			DTaP	DTaP	Td	
H. Influenzae type b			Hib	Hib	Hib		Hib				
Polio			IPV	IPV	Polio				Polio		
Rotavirus			Rv	Rv	Rv						
Measles, Mumps, Rubella						MMR			MMR	(MMR)	
Varicella							Var			(Var)	

Approved by the Advisory Committee on Immunization Practices (ACIP), the American Academy of Pediatrics (AAP), and the American Academy of Family Physicians (AAFP). From the Centers for Disease Control and Prevention.

(From Marotz, Cross, & Rush (2001). *Health, Safety, and Nutrition for the Young Child*, 5E, Delmar.)

Developmental Checklists

A simple checklist, one for each child, is a useful observation tool for anyone working with infants and young children. Questions on the checklists that follow can be answered during the course of a child's everyday activities and over a period of a week or more. "No" answers signal further investigation may be in order. Several "no" answers indicate that additional investigation is a necessity.

The "sometimes" category is an important one. It suggests what the child can do, at least part of the time, or under some circumstances. The "sometimes" category provides space where brief notes and comments can be recorded about how and when a behavior occurs. In many cases, a child may simply need more practice, incentive, or adult encouragement. Hunches often provide a good starting point for working with the child. Again, if "sometimes" is checked a number of times, further investigation is recommended.

The observation checklists may be duplicated and used as part of the assessment process. A completed checklist contains information about a child that members of a developmental team would find useful in evaluating a child's development status and in determining an intervention program.

Child's Name _____   Age _____

Observer _____   Date _____

DEVELOPMENTAL CHECKLIST

BY SIX MONTHS: Does the child . . .	Yes	No	Sometimes
Show continued gains in height, weight, and head circumference?			
Reach for toys or objects when they are presented?			
Begin to roll from stomach to back?			
Sit with minimal support?			
Transfer objects from one hand to the other?			
Raise up on arms, lifting head and chest, when placed on stomach?			
Babble, coo, and imitate sounds?			
Turn to locate the source of a sound?			
Focus on an object and follow its movement vertically and horizontally?			
Exhibit a blink reflex?			
Enjoy being held and cuddled?			
Recognize and respond to familiar faces?			
Begin sleeping six to eight hours through the night?			
Suck vigorously when it is time to eat?			
Enjoy playing in water during bathtime?			

Child's Name _____   Age _____

Observer _____   Date _____

DEVELOPMENTAL CHECKLIST

BY TWELVE MONTHS: Does the child . . .	Yes	No	Sometimes
Walk with assistance?			
Roll a ball in imitation of an adult?			
Pick objects up with thumb and forefinger?			
Transfer objects from one hand to the other?			
Pick up dropped toys?			
Look directly at adult's face?			
Imitate gestures: peek-a-boo, bye-bye, pat-a-cake?			
Find object hidden under a cup?			
Feed self crackers (munching, not sucking on them)?			
Hold cup with two hands; drink with assistance?			
Smile spontaneously?			
Pay attention to own name?			
Respond to "no"?			
Respond differently to strangers and familiar persons?			
Respond differently to sounds: vacuum, phone, door?			
Look at person who speaks to him or her?			
Respond to simple directions accompanied by gestures?			
Make several consonant–vowel combination sounds?			
Vocalize back to person who has talked to him or her?			
Use intonation patterns that sound like scolding, asking, exclaiming?			
Say "da-da" or "ma-ma"?			

Child's Name _____   Age _____

Observer _____   Date _____

DEVELOPMENTAL CHECKLIST

BY TWO YEARS: Does the child . . .	Yes	No	Sometimes
Walk alone?			
Bend over and pick up toy without falling over?			
Seat self in child-size chair? Walk up and down stairs with assistance?			
Place several rings on a stick?			
Place five pegs in a pegboard?			
Turn pages two or three at a time?			
Scribble?			
Follow one-step direction involving something familiar: "Give me _____." "Show me _____." "Get a _____."?			
Match familiar objects?			
Use spoon with some spilling?			
Drink from cup holding it with one hand, unassisted?			
Chew food?			
Take off coat, shoe, sock?			
Zip and unzip large zipper?			
Recognize self in mirror or picture?			
Refer to self by name?			
Imitate adult behaviors in play—for example, feeds "baby"?			
Help put things away?			
Respond to specific words by showing what was named: toy, pet, family member?			
Ask for desired items by name: (cookie)?			
Answer with name of object when asked "What's that"?			
Make some two-word statements: "Daddy bye-bye"?			

Child's Name _____   Age _____

Observer _____   Date _____

DEVELOPMENTAL CHECKLIST

BY THREE YEARS: Does the child . . .	Yes	No	Sometimes
Run well in a forward direction?			
Jump in place, two feet together?			
Walk on tiptoe?			
Throw ball (but without direction or aim)? Kick ball forward?			
String four large beads?			
Turn pages in book singly?			
Hold crayon: imitate circular, vertical, horizontal strokes?			
Match shapes?			

Demonstrate number concepts of 1 and 2?
  (Can select 1 or 2; can tell if one or two
  objects.)			

Use spoon without spilling?			
Drink from a straw?			
Put on and take off coat?			
Wash and dry hands with some assistance?			
Watch other children; play near them; sometimes join in their play?			
Defend own possessions?			

Use symbols in play—for example, tin pan on
  head becomes helmet and crate becomes a
  spaceship?			

Respond to "Put _____ in the box," "Take the _____ out of the box"?			
Select correct item on request: big versus little; one versus two?			

Identify objects by their use: show own shoe
  when asked, "What do you wear on
  your feet?"			

Ask questions?			

Tell about something with functional phrases
  that carry meaning: "Daddy go airplane."
  "Me hungry now"?			

Child's Name _____   Age _____

Observer _____   Date _____

DEVELOPMENTAL CHECKLIST

BY FOUR YEARS: Does the child . . .	Yes	No	Sometimes
Walk on a line?			
Balance on one foot briefly? Hop on one foot?			
Jump over an object 6 inches high and land on both feet together?			
Throw ball with direction?			
Copy circles and X's?			
Match six colors?			
Count to 5?			
Pour well from pitcher? Spread butter, jam with knife?			
Button, unbutton large buttons?			
Know own sex, age, last name?			
Use toilet independently and reliably?			
Wash and dry hands unassisted?			
Listen to stories for at least five minutes?			
Draw head of person and at least one other body part?			
Play with other children?			
Share, take turns (with some assistance)?			
Engage in dramatic and pretend play?			
Respond appropriately to "Put it beside," "Put it under"?			
Respond to two-step directions: "Give me the sweater and put the shoe on the floor"?			
Respond by selecting the correct object—for example, hard versus soft object?			
Answer "if," "what," and "when" questions?			
Answer questions about function: "What are books for"?			

Child's Name _____   Age _____

Observer _____   Date _____

DEVELOPMENTAL CHECKLIST

BY FIVE YEARS:
Does the child . . .
Walk backward, heel to toe?
Walk up and down stairs, alternating feet?
Cut on line?
Print some letters?
Point to and name three shapes?
Group common related objects: shoe, sock,
    and foot: apple, orange, and plum?
Demonstrate number concepts to 4 or 5?
Cut food with a knife: celery, sandwich?
Lace shoes?
Read from story picture book—in other words,
    tell story by looking at pictures?
Draw a person with three to six body parts?
Play and interact with other children; engage
    in dramatic play that is close to reality?
Build complex structures with blocks or other
    building materials?
Respond to simple three-step directions: "Give
    me the pencil, put the book on the table,
    and hold the comb in your hand"?
Respond correctly when asked to show penny,
    nickel, and dime?
Ask "How" questions?
Respond verbally to "Hi" and "How are you"?
Tell about event using past and future tenses?
Use conjunctions to string words and phrases
    together—for example, "I saw a bear and a
    zebra and a giraffe at the zoo"?
	Yes	No	Sometimes

Child's Name _____   Age _____

Observer _____   Date _____

DEVELOPMENTAL CHECKLIST

BY SIX YEARS: Does the child . . .	Yes	No	Sometimes
Walk across a balance beam?			
Skip with alternating feet?			
Hop for several seconds on one foot?			
Cut out simple shapes?			
Copy own first name?			
Show well-established handedness; demonstrate consistent right- or left-handedness?			
Sort objects on one or more dimensions: color, shape, or function?			
Name most letters and numerals?			
Count by rote to 10; know what number comes next?			
Dress self completely; tie bows?			
Brush teeth unassisted?			
Have some concept of clock time in relation to daily schedule?			
Cross street safely?			
Draw a person with head, trunk, legs, arms, and features; often add clothing details?			
Play simple board games?			
Engage in cooperative play with other children, involving group decisions, role assignments, rule observance?			
Use construction toys, such as Legos, blocks, to make recognizable structures?			
Do fifteen-piece puzzles?			
Use all grammatical structures: pronouns, plurals, verb tenses, conjunctions?			
Use complex sentences: carry on conversations?			

Child's Name _____   Age _____

Observer _____   Date _____

DEVELOPMENTAL CHECKLIST

BY SEVEN YEARS: Does the child . . . Concentrate on completing puzzles and board games? Ask many questions? Use correct verb tenses, word order, and sentence structure in conversation? Correctly identify right and left hands? Make friends easily? Show some control of anger, using words instead of physical aggression? Participate in play that requires teamwork and rule observance? Seek adult approval for efforts? Enjoy reading and being read to? Use pencil to write words and numbers? Sleep undisturbed through the night? Catch a tennis ball, walk across balance beam, hit ball with bat? Plan and carry out simple projects with minimal adult help? Tie own shoes? Draw pictures with greater detail and sense of proportion? Care for own personal needs with some adult supervision? Wash hands? Brush teeth? Use toilet? Dress self? Show some understanding of cause-and-effect concepts?	Yes	No	Sometimes

Child's Name _____   Age _____

Observer _____   Date _____

DEVELOPMENTAL CHECKLIST

BY EIGHT AND NINE YEARS: Does the child . . .	Yes	No	Sometimes
Have energy to play, continuing growth, few illnesses?			
Use pencil in a deliberate and controlled manner?			
Express relatively complex thoughts in a clear and logical fashion?			
Carry out multiple four- to five-step instructions?			
Become less easily frustrated with own performance?			
Interact and play cooperatively with other children?			
Show interest in creative expression—telling stories, jokes, writing, drawing, singing?			
Use eating utensils with ease?			
Have a good appetite? Show interest in trying new foods?			
Know how to tell time?			
Have control of bowel and bladder functions?			
Participate in some group activities—games, sports, plays?			
Want to go to school? Seem disappointed if must miss a day?			
Demonstrate beginning skills in reading, writing, and math?			
Accept responsibility and complete work independently?			
Handle stressful situations without becoming overly upset?			

Child's Name _____   Age _____

Observer _____   Date _____

DEVELOPMENTAL CHECKLIST

BY TEN AND ELEVEN YEARS: Does the child . . .	Yes	No	Sometimes
Continue to increase in height and weight?			
Exhibit improving coordination: running, climbing, riding a bike, writing?			
Handle stressful situations without becoming overly upset or violent?			
Construct sentences using reasonably correct grammar: nouns, adverbs, verbs, adjectives?			
Understand concepts of time, distance, space, volume?			
Have one or two "best friends"?			
Maintain friendships over time?			
Approach challenges with a reasonable degree of self-confidence?			
Play cooperatively and follow group instructions?			
Begin to show an understanding of moral standards: right from wrong, fairness, honesty, good from bad?			
Look forward to, and enjoy, school?			
Appear to hear well and listen attentively?			
Enjoy reasonably good health, with few episodes of illness or health-related complaints?			
Have a good appetite and enjoy mealtimes?			
Take care of own personal hygiene without assistance?			
Sleep through the night, waking up refreshed and energetic?			

Child's Name _____   Age _____

Observer _____   Date _____

DEVELOPMENTAL CHECKLIST

BY TWELVE AND THIRTEEN YEARS: Does the child . . .	Yes	No	Sometimes
Appear to be growing: increasing height and maintaining a healthy weight (not too thin or too heavy)?			
Understand changes associated with puberty or have an opportunity to learn and ask questions?			
Complain of headaches or blurred vision?			
Have an abnormal posture or curving of the spine?			
Seem energetic and not chronically fatigued?			
Stay focused on a task and complete assignments?			
Remember and carry out complex instructions?			
Sequence, order, and classify objects?			
Use longer and more complex sentence structure?			
Engage in conversation; tell jokes and riddles?			
Enjoy playing organized games and team sports?			
Respond to anger-invoking situations without resorting to violence or physical aggression?			
Begin to understand and solve complex mathematical problems?			
Accept blame for actions on most occasions?			
Enjoy competition?			
Accept and carry out responsibility in a dependable manner?			
Go to bed willingly and wake up refreshed?			
Take pride in appearance; keep self reasonably clean?			

Child Health History

 SAMPLE FORM

The information provided on this form is only intended to serve as a guideline. You are encouraged to modify the questions according to the needs and goals of your individual program.

 GENERAL INFORMATION

1. Child's Name _____   _____
   (First)   (Last)

2. Child's Address _____
   (Street)

   _____
   (City, State, Zip)

3. Home Telephone Number   (____)_____

4. Child's Gender: _____ Female _____ Male

5. Child's Date of Birth _____ _____ _____
   Month   Date   Year

6. Mother's Name _____

7. Father's Name _____

BIRTH HISTORY

8. Length of Pregnancy: ___ 6 ___ 7 ___ 8 ___ 9 months

9. Child's weight at birth: ___ lbs. ___ ozs. or ___ kilograms

10. Were there any unusual factors or complications during this pregnancy? ___ yes ___ no. Please describe: _____

11. Did your child have any medical problems at birth? i.e., jaundice, difficulty breathing, birth defects ___ yes ___ no. Please describe: _____
    _____

12. Which doctor is most familiar with your child? _____
    doctor's telephone number: (___) _____

13. Does your child take any medications on a regular basis? ___ yes ___ no.
    If yes, name of medication and dosage: _____

14. Has your child had any of the following illnesses (dates)?

    ___ measles   ___ rheumatic fever

    ___ mumps   ___ chicken pox

    ___ whooping cough   ___ pneumonia

    ___ middle ear infection   ___ hepatitis
        (otitis media)

    ___ meningitis

15. Where there any complications with these illnesses, such as high fever, convulsions, muscle weaknesses, and so on? ___ yes ___ no. Please describe: _____

16. Has your child ever been hospitalized? ___ yes ___ no.
    Number of times ___ Total length of time _____
    Reasons: _____

17. Has your child had any other serious illness or injuries that did not involve hospitalization? ___ yes ___ no. Please describe:_____
    _____

18. How many colds has your child had during the past year? _____

19. Does your child have:

    Allergies? ___ yes ___ no. (please specify which allergies):

    Foods _____

    Animals _____

    Medicine _____

    Asthma? ___ yes ___ no

    Hayfever? ___ yes ___ no

20. Has your child had any problems with earaches or ear infections?

    ___ yes ___ no If yes, how often in the past year? _____

21. Has your child's hearing been tested? ___ yes ___ no

    Date of test: _____ _____
                    (month)   (year)

    Was there any evidence of hearing loss? ___ yes ___ no

    If yes, describe: _____

22. Does your child currently have tubes in his or her ears? ___ yes ___ no

23. Do you have any concerns about your child's speech or language

    development? ___ yes ___ no. If yes, describe:_____

24. Has your child's vision been tested? ___ yes ___ no

    Date of test: _____ _____
                    (month)   (year)

25. Was there any evidence of vision loss? ___ yes ___ no

    Please describe: _____

26. Does your child do some things that you find troublesome?

    Please describe: _____

27. Has your child ever participated in out-of-the-home child care services—for

    example, sitter, day care, preschool? ___ yes ___ no. Please describe:

    _____

CHILD'S PLAY ACTIVITIES

28. Where does your child usually play—for example, backyard, kitchen, bedroom? _____

29. Does your child usually play: ___ alone? ___ with one to two other children? ___ with brothers/sisters? ___ with older children? ___ with younger children? ___ with children of the same age?

30. Is your child usually ___ cooperative? ___ shy? ___ aggressive?

31. What are some of your child's favorite toys and activities?
    Please describe: _____

32. Are there any particular behaviors you would like us to watch?
    Please describe: _____

    _____

CHILD'S DAILY ROUTINE

33. Do you have any concerns about your child's:

    ___ eating habits?

    ___ sleeping habits?

    ___ toilet training?

    If yes, please describe: _____

34. Is your child toilet trained? ___ yes ___ no. If yes, how often does your child have an accident? _____

35. What word(s) does your child use or understand for:
    urination _____ bowel movement _____

36. How many hours does your child sleep? At night _____?
    Goes to bed at: ___ P.M. Wakes up at: ___ A.M. Afternoon nap:_____

37. When your child is upset, how do you comfort him or her? _____

    _____

38. The term *family* has many different meanings. Since the topic of families and family members is often included in classroom discussions, please list or describe who your child considers to be "family" at home. _____

_____

39. How many brothers and (or) sisters does your child have?

   Brothers (ages): _____   Sisters (ages): _____

   _____   _____

   _____   _____

40. What language(s) is/(are) most commonly spoken in your home?

   English _____   Other _____

41. Is there any additional information that would help us understand or work more effectively with your child? _____

_____

Assessment Instruments

 EXAMPLES OF SCREENING TESTS

AGS Early Screening Profiles test children two to seven years of age for cognitive, language, social, self-help, and motor skills; includes information provided by parents, teachers, and child care providers.

Denver Developmental Screening Test (Denver II) is appropriate for testing children from birth to six years of age in four developmental areas: personal-social, language, fine motor, and gross motor. Ratings of the child's behavior during testing can be recorded.

Developmental Activities Screening Inventory (DASI II) screens children one month to five years; a nonverbal test especially useful for children with hearing or language disorders; also offers adaptations for children with vision problems.

Developmental Indicators for the Assessment of Learning—Revised (DIAL-R) is designed to screen children two years to five years, nine months, in motor, concept, and language development; includes a checklist of social-emotional behaviors observed during testing. A Parent Information Form related to child's health and home–school experiences is part of the kit.

First Steps: Screening Test for Evaluating Preschoolers can be used with children two years, nine months, to six years, two months, on cognitive, communication, and motor skills; an Adaptive Behavior Checklist and a Social-Emotional Scale is included as well as a Parent–Teacher Scale related to the child's behavior at home and at school.

EXAMPLES OF ASSESSMENT INSTRUMENTS

APGAR Scoring System is administered at one minute and again at five minutes after birth; the APGAR assesses muscle tone, respiration, color, heart beat, and reflexes for a maximum score of 10. The information is used to determine which infants need special care.

Assessment, Evaluation, and Programming Systems (AEPS) for Infants and Children (volumes 1–2, birth to three; volumes 3–4, three to six years) is an authentic, family-friendly system for assessing very young children. It ties together assessment outcomes with early intervention strategies that are activity-based and family-centered.

Audiology, that is, hearing assessment of infants and children, requires clinical testing by a trained technician. It is *imperative,* however, in terms of early identification, that teachers and parents record and report their observations whenever they suspect a child is not hearing well. Warning signs include:

- pulling or banging on an ear
- drainage from ear canal
- failing to respond or looking puzzled when spoken to
- requesting frequent repetitions—What? Huh?
- speaking in too loud or too soft of a voice
- articulating or discriminating sounds poorly

Bayley Scales of Infant Development evaluate both motor and cognitive development. The age range has been expanded to cover children from one month to three-and-one-half years. The Mental Scales and the Motor Scales are separate instruments.

Brigance Diagnostic Inventory of Early Development is designed to assess children, birth to six years, in multiple developmental domains: psychomotor, speech and language, knowledge and comprehension, self-help, and pre-academic skills.

Early Childhood Environment Rating Scale (ECERS) provides a comprehensive assessment of the classroom environment: space, materials, activities, supervision, child–child and adult–child interactions. Useful in infant, toddler, and preschool settings.

Home Observation for Measurement of the Environment (HOME) is the best known and most widely used of in-home inventories. Scales range from infancy to middle childhood; each version assesses the physical environment as well as the social, emotional, and cognitive support available to the child.

Kaufman Assessment Battery for Children is used with children from two-and-one-half to twelve years of age to test mental processing abilities. The test items are designed to minimize the effects of verbal, gender, and ethnic bias.

Kaufman Survey of Early Academic and Language Skills assesses three- to six-year-olds' reception and expressive language skills as well as concepts related to numbers, counting, letters, and words; includes an articulation survey.

Learning Accomplishment Profile—Diagnostic Standardized Assessment (LAP-D) assesses children two-and-one-half through age six on fine motor (writing and manipulative skills), gross motor (such as body and object movement), matching and counting (viewed as cognitive tasks), and language skills (comprehension and object naming).

Neonatal Behavioral Assessment Scale (NBAS—often referred to as *The Brazelton*) assesses behavioral responses in full-term infants up to twenty-eight days of age. A significant modification of the NBAS is the *Kansas Supplement (NBAS-K)*. It adds a number of critical parameters and also assesses the infant's typical behavior (state) as well as optimal behavior (the only focus of the original NBAS).

Peabody Developmental Motor Scales evaluate children from birth through seven years of age in fine motor (grasping, eye–hand coordination, and manual dexterity) and gross motor development (reflexes, balance, locomotion, throwing, and catching).

Peabody Picture Vocabulary Test—Revised can be used with children age three into adulthood; it is a test of receptive language with an adaptation for individuals with motor impairments; a Spanish-language version is available.

Preschool Language Scale assesses children one to three years of age on auditory comprehension, articulation, grammatical forms, and basic concept development.

The Snellen E or *Illiterate E* test is an instrument commonly used for assessing the visual acuity of young children (knowing the alphabet is not required). As with hearing, screening of young children for vision problems relies heavily on parents' and teachers' informal observations and telltale signs such as:

- rubbing eyes frequently or closing or covering one eye
- constantly stumbling over, or running into, things
- complaining of frequent headaches
- blinking excessively when looking at books or reading
- brushing hand over eyes as if trying to get rid of a blur

Infants and toddlers are obviously too young to be evaluated in this fashion. However, their vision can be assessed through informal techniques, such as:

- observing the infant's ability to focus on an object
- watching for uncoordinated eye movements, such as crossed or wandering eyes
- checking for a blink reflex

■ seeing if the infant can visually follow (track) an object, such as a toy, as it is moved in a 180 arc

Work Sampling System (WSS) is a unique approach for documenting authentic and ongoing evaluation of children's developmental progress; it uses a combination of portfolio development (with samples of child's work) and checklists for data collection. Assessments are conducted three times during the course of a year, and provide teachers with feedback on effective instructional strategies, as well as how children are responding. Appropriate for children, preschool to fifth grade.

Resources for Families and Professionals

Many resources are available to families, teachers, and service providers who work with young children. These resources are provided at the community, state, and national levels and fall into two major categories: direct services and information sources.

DIRECT SERVICES

Developmental screenings are available through a number of local agencies and organizations. In addition, most communities offer an array of services and programs designed to help families cope with and meet the special needs and challenges of caring for a child with developmental disabilities. Some agencies also provide technical assistance to educators and other professionals who are working with these children. Often, the agencies themselves serve as a valuable resource because they are familiar with other community-based services, assistance programs, and trained specialists.

Examples of community services and resources for families:

- Child Find screening programs
- Interagency Coordinating Councils (ICCs)
- Early childhood centers and therapeutic programs for exceptional children
- Public health departments at city, county, and state levels
- Local public school districts, especially the special services divisions
- Hospitals, medical centers, and well-child clinics

- University-Affiliated Programs (UAPs)
- Head Start and Even Start programs
- Mental health centers
- State-supported low-cost health insurance for children
- Parent support groups
- Service groups that provide **respite care**, transportation, or financial assistance
- Marriage counseling programs
- Philanthropic organizations, such as the Lion's Club (glasses), Shriners, Make a Wish Foundation
- Professional practitioners: pediatricians, nurses, psychologists, audiologists, ophthalmologists, early childhood specialists, educators, speech-language therapists, occupational and physical therapists, and social workers

Examples of national and professional organizations:

There are also many national organizations that offer extensive information, as well as direct assistance to children and families with specific needs. Contact information can usually be found in local telephone directories, the *Encyclopedia of Associations* (at the library), or on the Internet. For example,

- Allergy and Asthma Foundation www.aafa.org
- American Council for the Blind www.acb.org
- American Diabetes Association www.diabetes.org
- The American Foundation for the Blind www.afb.org
- American Heart Association www.americanheart.org
- American Society for Deaf Children www.deafchildren.org
- The Autism Society of America www.autism-society.org
- Children's Craniofacial Association www.ccakids.org
- Cleft Palate Foundation www.cleftline.org
- Council for Exceptional Children www.cec.sped.org
- Down Syndrome Children www.downsnet.org
- Epilepsy Foundation of America www.efa.org
- Learning Disabilities Association www.ldanatl.org
- National Down Syndrome Society www.ndss.org
- National Easter Seals www.easter-seals.org
- The United States Cerebral Palsy Athletic Association www.uscpaa.org

Examples of technical assistance programs:

There are also a number of programs and organizations whose purpose is to provide direct, technical assistance to educational programs and agencies serving young

---

respite care—child care assistance given to families to allow them temporary relief from the demands of caring for a disabled child.

children with developmental disabilities. Many of these groups also offer instructional material. A sample of such agencies includes:

■ American Printing House for the Blind www.aph.org. This group produces materials and services for children with visual impairments, including talking books, magazines in braille, and large-type books, as well as materials intended for educators of blind or visually impaired children.

■ Head Start Resource Access Projects (RAPs). Their purpose is to assist Head Start programs in providing comprehensive services to children with developmental problems.

■ National Early Childhood-Technical Assistance System (NEC-TAS) www. nectas.unc.org. This agency provides many types of assistance to federally funded projects for children with disabilities.

■ National Information Center for Children and Youth with Disabilities www. nichcy.org.

INFORMATION SOURCES

A wealth of information is published for parents, teachers, and professionals who work with children with developmental problems. Many professional journals, government publications, CD-ROMs, and reference books are available in most public and university libraries. Special interest groups and professional organizations also produce a wealth of printed materials focused on high-risk children and children with developmental delays.

Selected examples of information resources:

■ Professional journals and periodicals, such as the *Journal of the Division for Early Childhood, Topics in Early Childhood Special Education, Exceptional Children,* and *Teaching Exceptional Children, Child Development, Early Childhood Research Quarterly, Early Childhood Digest, Young Children.*

■ Trade magazines for parents, such as *Parents of Exceptional Children, Parenting,* and *Parents Magazine.*

■ Government documents, reports, and pamphlets. These cover almost any topic related to child development, child care, early intervention, nutrition, parenting, and specific developmental problems. Publications can be obtained through the Superintendent of Documents, U.S. Government Printing Office, Washington, DC 20402; many are available in local government buildings, including public libraries and on the Internet.

■ Bibliographic indexes and abstracts usually located in university, college, and large public libraries. These are particularly useful to students and practitioners who need to locate information quickly on a specific topic. Examples of several include:

- *The Review of Child Development*
- *Current Topics in Early Childhood Education*
- Electronic journals and serials, such as *Early Childhood Research & Practice, Networks* (on-line journal for teacher research), *Parent News, Contemporary Issues in Early Childhood, Future of Children, Health Child Care, Bulletin of the World Association of Early Childhood Educators*

Examples of professional organizations that focus on children's issues:

- American Academy of Pediatrics www.aap.org
- American Association on Mental Retardation (AAMR) www.aamr.org
- American Public Health Association www.apha.org
- American Speech, Language, Hearing Association (ASHA) www.asha.org
- Association for Retarded Citizens (ARC) www.thearc.org
- Children's Defense Fund www.childrensdefense.org
- Council for Exceptional Children (CEC), especially the Division for Early Childhood (DEC) within the Council www.cec.sped.org
- Early Childhood Resource Center www.rti.org
- Early Head Start National Resource Center www.ehsnrc.org
- Head Start Bureau www.acf.dhhs.gov/programs
- March of Dimes www.modimes.org
- National Association of Child Care Resource & Referral Agencies www.naccrra.org
- National Association for the Education of Young Children (NAEYC) www.naeyc.org
- National Association for Family Child Care www.assoc-mgmt.com/users.nafcc
- The National Information Center for Children and Youth with Disabilities www.nichcy.org
- National Parent Information Network (NPIN) http://ericps.ed.uiuc.edu/npin/npinhome.html
- National Parent Network on Disablties www.npnd.org
- Parents Helping Parents www.php.org
- Special Olympics International www.specialolympics.org

CONCLUSION

Finding help for children with developmental delays and disabilities is not a simple matter. The issues are often complex—some children present tangles of interrelated developmental problems that tend to multiply when not addressed during the crucial first five years of life. Therefore, effective intervention must begin early, and be comprehensive, integrated, ongoing and family-centered. It must also take into account multiple developmental areas at the same time. This effort requires teamwork on the part of specialists from many disciplines, service providers, and agencies working cooperatively with the child and the family. It also requires an awareness of legislative acts and public policies that affect services for children with developmental problems and their families, as well as available resources and effective means of collaboration. Only then will children and families fully benefit from an early intervention team approach.

Federal Legislation Related to Children and Families

- **PL 88-452 (1965).** A part of the 1960s anti-poverty movement, this law provided for the establishment of Head Start and its supplemental services such as developmental screening, medical and dental care, better nutrition, parent training, and early education for three- and four-year-olds living at or below the poverty level. The benefits for these children and their families have been documented conclusively over the years. Amendments to the law in 1972 and 1974 mandated that Head Start serve children with disabilities.

- **Early and Periodic Screening, Diagnosis, and Treatment Program (EPSDT) (1967).** This national program was added to Medicaid and was designed to locate and evaluate children at developmental risk for medical and psychological problems, and to also address family needs.

- **Supplemental Nutrition Program for Women, Infants, and Children (WIC) (1972).** This act created a program aimed at improving maternal health during pregnancy, promoting full-term fetal development, and increasing the birth weight of newborns. Medical supervision, food vouchers, and nutrition education are provided to low-income pregnant women and their children up to the age of five.

- **PL 94-142 (1975).** Originally called the Education for All Handicapped Children Act (EHA), this law was renamed the Individuals with Disabilities Education Act (IDEA) (PL 101-476) in 1990. A major intent of the act was to motivate states, through financial incentives, to provide comprehensive prevention, treatment, and Individualized Educational Plans (IEPs) for children three to five years old with, and at-risk for developmental problems.

■ PL 99-457 Education of the Handicapped Act Amendments (1986). These amendments to PL 94-142 are particularly noteworthy because they require states to provide comprehensive special education services to children with developmental disabilities and delays and to include their families through the Individualized Family Service Plan (IFSP). The acts also extended intervention programs to infants and toddlers (Part H); this portion of the bill is not mandatory and, therefore, not all states offer these services. Additional features of this legislation include an emphasis on multidisciplinary assessment, a designated service coordinator, a family-focused approach to a child's problems, and a system of service coordination.

■ PL101-336 Americans with Disabilities Act (ADA) (1990). This national civil rights law protects against discrimination on the basis of a disability. The intent is to remove barriers that interfere with full inclusion in every aspect of society—education, employment, and public services. Implications for children and their families are clear: child care programs are required to adapt their settings and programs to accommodate children with disabilities. In 1997 The Individuals With Disabilities Act Amendment (IDEA) significantly improved the educational opportunities for children with disabilities. IDEA 1997 focuses on teaching and learning, and established high expectations for disabled children to achieve real educational results.

■ Head Start legislation (1997). This legislation improves school readiness, family literacy, staff training, and credentialing, and increases monies for quality improvements.

Appendix

8

Annotated Bibliography and References

 ## CHILD DEVELOPMENT

Bee, H. (1999). *The developing child* (9th ed.). Boston, MA: Allyn & Bacon.
> This comprehensive child development text is highly readable. It provides psychologically sound, yet conversational, coverage of all aspects of child development. Throughout, research findings are reported in such a way that they are readily related to everyday home and school settings.

Berk, L. A. (1999). *Infants, children & adolescents* (3rd ed.). Boston, MA: Allyn & Bacon.
> The fundamentals of child development are presented in a clear and chronological manner. Many contemporary topics are addressed, with special emphasis on the influence of culture on children's development, the application of research to practice, and social policy as it affects children and families.

Berns, R. (1994). *Topical child development*. Clifton Park, NY: Delmar Learning.
> Written by a sensitive child developmentalist, this text combines psychological theory and research in ways that are delightfully descriptive and readily applicable to the lives of children (a topical approach).

Charlesworth, R. (2000) (5th ed.). *Understanding child development*. Clifton Park, NY: Delmar Learning.
> An excellent book for teachers and parents; the focus is on growth and development in the infant, toddler, and preschool child. A wealth of basic information is skillfully combined with numerous suggestions for working with young children.

Cobb, N. (2001). *The child*. Mountain View, CA: Mayfield.
> A comprehensive introductory textbook that examines development from prebirth through adolescence. The material addresses many contemporary social issues in a reader-friendly style.

237

Cole, M., & Cole, S. (2000). *The development of children*. New York: Scientific American Books.
   This child development text presents the fundamental theories and contemporary issues, inclusive of birth through adolescence, in a thorough and readable style with a strong emphasis on the influence of culture.

Flavell, J. H. (1992). *Cognitive development*. Englewood Cliffs, NJ: Prentice-Hall.
   No text on cognitive development can completely escape technical complexity, but this one, written by a leading researcher on cognitive development and developmental theory, is one of the best, yet least difficult, because of its easy, anecdotal style.

Fogel, A. (2000). *Infancy*. New York: Wadsworth.
   A comprehensive overview of child development, conception through age three, which examines a number of contemporary factors that influence individual differences, including intelligence, sociability, and temperament.

Santrock, J. W. (2000). *Children* (6th ed.). Dubuque, IA: Wm. C. Brown.
   An appealing and easily read textbook that addresses contemporary topics in child development in a culturally sensitive manner. Extensive research findings, with emphasis on everyday application, are incorporated throughout the book. Content covers birth through adolescence with an emphasis on parent education, culture, and gender influence.

OBSERVATION AND ASSESSMENT

Bentzen, W. R. (2001). *Seeing young children: A guide to observing and recording behavior* (4th ed.). Clifton Park, NY: Delmar Learning.
   A practical book on observing young children, recording their developmental progress, and using the information to foster each child's development in multiple areas.

Harrington, H., Meisels, S., McMahon, P., Dichtelmiller, M., & Jablon, J. (1997). *Observing, documenting, and assessing learning*. Ann Arbor, MI: Rebus.
   This workbook is designed to help students and teachers learn to conduct authentic performance-based assessments (Work Sampling System), prepare student portfolios, and use the outcomes for improving children's achievements. Seven domain areas are examined in the assessment: personal-social; language and literacy; mathematical thinking; scientific thinking; social studies; arts; physical development.

Hills, T. W. (1992). Reaching potentials through appropriate assessment. In S. Bradekamp & T. Rosegrant (Eds.), *Reaching potentials: Appropriate curriculum and assessment for young children* (vol. 1, pp. 43–63). Washington, DC: National Association for the Education of Young Children.
   The entire volume is worthwhile, with this particular essay pointing out how direct observation of children is a major source of information for designing both individual and group curriculum activities.

McAfee, O., & Leong, D. (1997). *Assessing and guiding young children's development and learning*. Boston, MA: Allyn & Bacon.
   This is an excellent book that covers authentic assessment and screening strategies in

easily understood detail; many examples are also included. The authors stress assessment as a process, sensitivity to individual differences, and professional responsibility.

McLean, M., Bailey, D., & Wolery, M. (1996). *Assessing infants and preschoolers with special needs* (2nd ed.). Columbus, OH: Prentice-Hall.
An excellent book written for early childhood educators and allied health professionals. The authors stress the importance of observation in natural settings, a family-centered approach, and sensitivity to cultural differences.

Mindes, G., Ireton, H., & Mardell-Czudnowski, C. (1996). *Assessing young children.* Clifton Park, NY: Delmar Learning.
This book provides valuable information about a range of assessment strategies, including a review of screening tools and suppliers. Emphasis is placed on the appropriate use of assessment findings for making sound decisions that affect young children and planning developmentally appropriate practices.

Nilsen, B. A. (2001). *Week by week: Observing and recording young children* (2nd ed). Clifton Park, NY: Delmar Learning.
The author presents a systematic yet feasible plan for documenting children's behavior. Various methods of observing and recording are featured along with principles of child development and appropriate classroom practices. Teacher trainers, practicum students, and classroom teachers will find this text most useful.

Venn, J. (2000). *Assessing students with special needs.* Upper Saddle River, NJ: Merrill.
An excellent book that includes easy-to-understand explanations of basic statistical concepts needed for interpreting assessment testing outcomes. The author also provides extensive descriptions of the full range of assessment options and instruments including the pros, cons, and limitations of each.

 ## CHILDREN WITH SPECIAL NEEDS

Allen, K. E., & Schwartz, I. (2001). *The exceptional child: Inclusion in early childhood education* (4th ed.). Clifton Park, NY: Delmar Learning.
A comprehensive text based on developmental principles as they apply to the inclusion and appropriate education of children of all developmental capabilities in early childhood programs.

Bagnato, S., Neisworth, J., & Munson, S. (1997). *Linking assessment and early intervention.* Baltimore, MD: Brookes.
Detailed descriptions of numerous assessment instruments and approaches are discussed in this book. Emphasis is placed on how to use evaluative information for planning individualized program development, particularly in early intervention settings.

Blackman, J. A. (1997). *Medical aspects of developmental disabilities in children birth through three.* Rockville, MD: Aspen Systems.
A highly recommended book for early childhood personnel; it provides well-illustrated and readily understood information about medical issues that affect the developmental progress of young children.

Hanson, M., & Harris, S. (1986). *Teaching the young child with motor delays.* Austin, TX: Pro-Ed.

An easy-to-read book bridging the gap between parents and clinicians working with children birth to age three with motor impairments; includes teaching strategies and therapy activities that can be used in the home and child care programs.

Johnson, L. J., & Gallagher, R. J. (1997). *Meeting early intervention challenges.* Baltimore: Brookes.

Written by noted professionals in the field, this book examines key issues and challenges associated with early intervention services for young children and their families. A strong commitment to professional collaboration and a transdisciplinary team approach is evident throughout the book.

Fuller, M., & Olsen, G. (1998). *Home-school relations.* Needham Heights, MA: Allyn & Bacon.

An excellent introduction to the fundamental principles underlying effective parent involvement. Particularly good are the chapters on communication, educational law, and research-based parent involvement models. Many resources (e.g., videos, organizaitons, Web sites) are also provided.

Noonan, M. J., & McCormick, L. (1993). *Early intervention in natural environments.* Pacific Grove, CA: Brooks/Cole.

A superior text that responds to the federal mandate to serve infants and young children with developmental problems in the natural environment of the family's choice, using play and other developmentally appropriate activities and learning opportunities.

Roush, J., & Matkin, N. (Eds.). (1994). *Infants and toddlers with hearing loss: Family-centered assessment and intervention.* Baltimore, MD: York.

The authors present valuable information on various hearing disorders in young children and discuss assessment techniques that are appropriate and family-focused.

Swan, W. W., & Morgan, J. L. (1993). *Collaboration for comprehensive services for young children and their families.* Baltimore, MD: Brookes.

A hands-on book that includes useful advice on creating and improving local interagency collaboration systems; examines their role, organizational and procedural concerns, financing, how to facilitate collaboration, and outcome evaluation.

Zipper, I., Weil, M., & Rounds, K. (1996). *Service coordination for early intervention: Parents and professionals.* Cambridge, MA: Brookline.

Valuable resource information is provided in this book to help parents and professionals develop early intervention programs with a strong family focus. Many logistical concerns in establishing intervention services are discussed, including provider roles, fostering collaboration, evaluating outcomes, staffing, and developing sensitivity to individual differences.

DIVERSITY

deMelendez, W., & Ostertag, V. (2001). *Teaching young children in multicultural classrooms: Issues, concepts and strategies.* Clifton Park, NY: Delmar Learning.

The authors describe themselves as "newcomers" to America, but they obviously are not newcomers to the cultural diversity represented in schools and early childhood programs. This well-organized text lays out plans for developing a functional, multicultural curriculum. In addition, it provides an insightful perspective on the history as well as the future of multiculturalism in our schools and country.

Gordon, A., & Browne, K. W. (1996). *Guiding young children in a diverse society.* Boston, MA: Allyn & Bacon.
The text is based on the premise that sound developmental principles apply to all children, regardless of their cultural backgrounds. A counterpoint is also examined: that teachers must employ cultural sensitivity when parents challenge the traditional early childhood philosophy. A worthwhile examination of increasingly diverse views of early education.

Isenberg, J. P., & Jalongo, M. R. (Eds.). (1997). *Major issues and trends in early childhood education.* New York: Teachers College Press.
A series of articles in which the authors examine current issues and challenges in the field with respect to public policy, inclusion, diversity, family involvement, DAP, and assessment.

Lynch, E. W., & Hanson, M. J. (1998). *Developing cross-cultural competence: A guide to working with young children and their families.* Baltimore, MD: Brookes.
Cultural, language, and developmental diversity among children and their families is the focus of this well-researched text. Chapters 4–11 offer detailed insights into seven of the most common cultures represented in schools and child care centers today. Cultural differences are described and analyzed by the authors, each native to their respective culture.

McCracken, J. B. (1993). *Valuing diversity: The primary years.* Washington, DC: NAEYC.
A good resource book that highlights the importance of recognizing and implementing practices that embrace individual differences.

 # PARENTING

Beer, W. R. (1992). *American stepfamilies.* New Brunswick, NJ: Transaction.
The author presents an overview of special concerns that face stepfamilies, particularly adult relationships and parent–child interactions. Extensive use of case histories and personal experiences lends a unique and sensitive insight into an often misunderstood family patterns.

Brooks, J. B. (1998). *The process of parenting.* Mountain View, CA: Mayfield.
A comprehensive book that addresses many contemporary parenting issues. Information on behavior management and developmentally appropriate expectations are included for children at all stages along the developmental continuum. Special attention is also given to issues of working parents, the single parent, stepparenting, and children with specific needs.

Christopherson, E. R. (1998). *Beyond discipline: Parenting that lasts a lifetime* (2nd ed.). Kansas City, KS: Westport.

This respected authority on child development and behavior management tackles a universal concern of parents and teachers with his usual wit and humor. His techniques have evolved from extensive research and years of clinical experience with young children.

Eisenberg, A., Murkoff, H., & Hathway, S. (1996). *What to expect: The first year.* New York: Workman.

Eisenberg, A., Murkoff, H., & Hathway, S. (1996). *What to expect: The toddler years.* New York: Workman.

Both of these books provide a wealth of down-to-earth information about very young children for new, as well as experienced, parents and caregivers. Excellent coverage of child development and caregiving routines is provided in an easy-to-understand manner. These just may be the baby owner's manuals that every parent searches for.

Hamner, T., & Turner, P. (2000). *Parenting in contemporary society.* Needham Heights, MA: Allyn & Bacon.

Examines the diversity of traditional and nontraditional family patterns in the United States, along with cultural differences, socioeconomic variations, working families, high-risk families, and adoption and foster care, as well as families of exceptional children. Throughout this book, emphasis is placed on effective parenting strategies.

Jaffe, M. L. (1997). *Understanding parenting.* New York: Wm. C. Brown.

A review focus is on child-rearing problems that typically confront parents and teachers of young children through adolescents. The importance of good parent–child relationships and communication is stressed throughout the text.

Marotz, L., Cross, M., & Rush, J. (2001). *Health, safety, and nutrition for the young child* (5th ed.). Clifton Park, NY: Delmar Learning.

A comprehensive overview of the numerous factors that enhance children's growth and development. It includes some of the most current research information and knowledge concerning each of these areas, and is especially useful for parents and teachers.

Parenting: An ecological perspective. (1993). T. Luster & L. Okagaki (Eds.). Hillsdale, NJ: Erlbaum.

An up-to-date compilation of research findings on a variety of contemporary issues related to differences in parenting behavior. These multidisciplinary studies were undertaken in an effort to improve the understanding of parental behavior and how to effectively enhance parent–child relationships.

Slonim, M. (1991). *Children, culture, and ethnicity.* New York: Garland.

The author examines how culture and ethnicity affect children's development, and provides in-depth descriptions of Asian, Hispanic American, African American, and European cultures. This book is a valuable resource for anyone who works with diverse populations.

Watson, L., Watson, M., & Wilson, L. C. (2003). *Infants and toddlers* (5th ed.). Clifton Park, NY: Delmar Learning.

Parents and teachers will find this book particularly useful in understanding developmental sequences, creating enriching environments, and providing appropriate learning experiences for infants and toddlers based on their developmental needs.

Weiser, M. (1991). *Infant/toddler care and education.* New York: Merrill.
Another comprehensive book that focuses on the major aspects of care and educational approaches unique to the infant and toddler. This book is designed for parents and teachers of children under three years of age.

Glossary

A

achievement tests—tests used to measure a child's academic progress (what has been learned).

acquisition—the process of learning or achieving objectives (e.g., walking, counting, reading).

amniocentesis—genetic screening procedure in which a needle is inserted through the mother's abdomen into the sac of fluid surrounding the fetus to detect abnormalities, such as Down syndrome or spina bifida; usually performed between the twelfth and sixteenth weeks.

at-risk—term describing children who may be more likely to have developmental problems due to certain predisposing factors, such as low birth weight, neglect, or maternal drug addiction.

B

bilateral—affecting both sides, as in loss of hearing in both ears.

binocular vision—both eyes working together, sending a single visual image to the brain.

bonding—the establishment of a close, loving relationship between an infant and an adult, usually the mother and father; also called *attachment*.

C

cephalocaudal—bone and muscular development that proceeds from head to toe.

Child Find—screening program designed to locate children with developmental problems through improved public awareness.

chronological—events or dates in sequence in the passage of time.

conception—the joining of a single egg or ovum from the female and a single sperm from the male.

concrete operational thought—Piaget's third stage of cognitive development; period when concepts of conservation and classification are understood.

conservation—the stage in children's cognitive development when they understand that an object's physical qualities (e.g., weight, mass) remain the same despite changes in its appearance; for example, flattening a ball of playdough does not affect its weight.

continuum—a continuous pathway; an event following a preceding event.

cumulative—an add-on process, bit by bit or step by step.

CVS—chorionic villus sampling; a genetic screening procedure in which a needle is inserted and cells removed from the outer layer of the placenta; performed between the eighth and twelfth weeks to detect some genetic disorders, such as Down syndrome.

D

deciduous teeth—initial set of teeth that eventually fall out; often referred to as "baby teeth."

depth perception—ability to determine the relative distance of objects from the observer.

descriptive praise—words or actions that describe to a child specifically what she or he is doing correctly or well.

development—refers to an increase in complexity, from simple to more complicated and detailed.

developmental integration—process of organizing and combining developmental skills that gradually allows the accomplishment of increasingly complex tasks.

developmental sequence—a continuum of predictable steps along a developmental pathway of skill achievement.

developmental team—a team of qualified professionals such as special educators, speech pathologists, occupational therapists, social workers, audiologists, nurses, and physical therapists, who evaluate a child's developmental progress and, together, prepare an intervention plan that addresses the child's special needs.

developmentally appropriate—a term used to describe learning experiences that are individualized based on a child's level of skills, abilities, and interests.

dysfluency—repetition of whole words or phrases uttered without frustration and often at the beginning of a statement ("let's go, let's go get some cookies").

E

ecological—interrelationships between each living thing and the environments in which it functions.

ecology—in terms of children's development, refers to interactive effects between children and their family, child care situation, school, and everything in the wider community that affects their lives.

embryo—the cell mass from the time of implantation through the eighth week of pregnancy.

essential needs—refers to basic physical needs, such as food, shelter, and safety as well as psychological needs, such as love, security, and trust, required for survival and healthy development.

F

Family Service Coordinator—an individual who serves as a family's advocate and assists them with identifying, locating, and making final arrangements with community services.

fine motor skills—also referred to as manipulative skills; includes stacking blocks, buttoning and zipping, and toothbrushing.

food jag—a period when only certain foods are preferred or accepted.

fontanels—small openings (sometimes called "soft spots") in the infant's skull bones, covered with soft tissue. Eventually they close.

functional language—language that allows children to get what they need or want.

G

gender—reference to being either male or female.

genes—genetic material that carries codes, or information, for all inherited characteristics.

gross motor—large muscle movements, such as locomotor skills (walking, skipping, swimming) and nonlocomotive movements (sitting, pushing, pulling, squatting).

growth—physical changes leading to an increase in size.

H

hand dominance—preference for using one hand over the other; most individuals are said to be either right- or left-handed.

head circumference—measurement of the head taken at its largest point (across forehead, around back of head, returning to the starting point).

heredity versus environment (nature/nurture) controversy—refers to whether development is primarily due to biological/genetic forces (heredity/nature) or to external forces (environment/nurture).

holophrastic speech—using a single word to express a complete thought.

I

implantation—the attachment of the blastocyst to the wall of the mother's uterus; occurs around the twelfth day.

inclusion programs—community child care, school, and recreational facilities in which all children from the most gifted to the most disabled participate in the same activities. Inclusion is a federal law mandated by the Congress of the United States. Originally, it was referred to as *mainstreaming*.

intelligible—language that can be understood by others.

interdependent—affecting or influencing development in other domains.

intermittent—anything that comes and goes at intervals.

intervention—treatment or special services for infants and young children; it needs to be provided as early as possible to prevent complications or delays in development.

intuition—thoughts or ideas based on feelings or a hunch.

in utero—the period when a fetus is developing in the mother's uterus.

J

jargon—unintelligible speech; in young children, it usually includes sounds and inflections of the native language.

L

linguistic code—verbal expression that has meaning to the child.

logic—process of reasoning based on a series of facts or events.

M

malocclusion—poor alignment of the upper and lower jaws and teeth; often called overbite.

multisensory—information received through more than one sense organ at a time.

N

neurological—refers to the brain and nervous system.

normal (typical) development—achievement of certain skills according to a fairly predictable sequence, although with many individual variations.

norms—age-level expectancies associated with the achievement of developmental skills.

nurturing—includes qualities of warmth, loving, caring, and attention to physical needs.

O

object permanence—Piaget's sensorimotor stage when infants understand that an object exists even when it is not in sight.

otitis media—a middle ear infection usually accompanied by pain and accumulation of fluid; most commonly experienced by children under age six.

P

proximodistal—bone and muscular development that begins closest to the trunk, gradually moving outward to the extremities.

pupil—the small, dark, central portion of the eye.

R

reciprocal—exchanges between individuals or groups that are mutually beneficial (or hindering).

refinement—progressive improvement in ability to perform fine and gross motor skills.

reflexive—movements resulting from impulses of the nervous system that cannot be controlled by the individual.

respite care—child care assistance given to families to allow them temporary relief from the demands of caring for a child with disabilities.

S

self-esteem—feelings about one's self-worth.

sensory information—information received through the senses: eyes, ears, nose, mouth, touch.

sonogram—visual image of the developing fetus created by directing high-frequency sound waves (ultrasound) at the mother's uterus; used to determine fetal age and physical abnormalities.

sphincter—the muscles necessary to accomplish bowel and bladder control.

stammering—to speak in an interrupted or repetitive pattern; not to be confused with stuttering.

strabismus—condition in which one or both eyes appear to be turned inward (crossed) or outward.

stranger anxiety—distress or fear shown when approached by unfamiliar persons.

T

teratogens—harmful agents that can cause fetal damage (e.g, malformations, neurological and behavioral problems) during the prenatal period.

tripod grasp—hand position, whereby an object, such as a pencil, is held between the thumb, first, and second fingers.

V

voluntary—movements that can be willed and purposively controlled and initiated by the individual.

Index

O

P